SRHE Working Party on Teaching Methods

Publication 1

Objectives in Higher Education

RUTH M. BEARD
F.G. HEALEY
P.J. HOLLOWAY

Second edition January 1974

Society for Research into Higher Education Ltd
25 Northampton Square London EC1V 0HL

Professor Ruth M. Beard is the holder of two degrees in Mathematics and two in Education. She has taught in grammar schools, a comprehensive school, a College of Education and two university Institutes of Education and has written articles and books for teachers at all levels. She is Professor of Educational Studies at the University of Bradford; she was formerly Senior Lecturer in Higher Education in charge of the University Teaching Methods Research Unit within the Department of Higher Education, University of London Institute of Education: the Leverhulme Trust financed the Unit between 1965 and 1968 and between 1968 and 1971 supported its research project investigating objectives in university teaching. Her publications include an SRHE monograph, now in its third edition, Research into teaching methods in higher education, in which teaching methods are discussed in relation to research findings, and Teaching and learning in higher education.

Professor F.G. HEALEY holds degrees in French Language and Literature of the University of Birmingham. He is Professor of French and Head of the Department of Linguistic and Regional Studies at the University of Surrey. He was formerly Head of the Department of Modern Languages at Portsmouth Polytechnic and before that was at the University of Manchester, Magee University College, Londonderry and the University of Birmingham. At Manchester University he was the leader of the University Education Research Project from 1964-1967. He has written books and articles on French history and literature, articles and papers on teaching methods, and a book on foreign language teaching in universities.

Dr. P.J. HOLLOWAY graduated in Dentistry from Guy's Hospital, London in 1949 and obtained his doctorate ten years later. He is Reader in Community Dentistry at the University of Manchester. He has held posts at the Medical Research Council, Harvard University and the University of London and was Reader in Children's Dentistry and Tutor to Dental Students at the University of Manchester. His main educational research interests are in the fields of professional examinations and clinical teaching methods and he has published many papers and articles on these subjects.

Reprinted February 1975

GENERAL INTRODUCTION TO THE SERIES

In the summer of 1966 the Society for Research into Higher Education organized a meeting for a small group of its members who had expressed an interest in studying methods of teaching relevant to higher education. Some of them were university teachers, anxious to improve their knowledge of educational theory. Others were research workers engaged in the experimental study of teaching methods, or in such fields as psychology, sociology and linguistics, who welcomed an opportunity to discuss their work with a more heterogeneous collection of interested colleagues than would normally have been easily accessible to them.

From this discussion group arose the Working Party on Teaching Methods in Higher Education, which has met on two or three occasions each term ever since.

Following a number of discussions, the group decided to plan and to write a book on teaching and learning in higher education. In view of the interests and expertise of the group they felt that this should be something more fundamental than 'tips for teachers' but that experimental evidence and theories should be considered where these were relevant. Further discussion convinced all members of the Working Party that it would be advantageous to define learning in terms of change in behaviour and to limit the use of the term 'education' so far as possible, for this is an emotive term lacking a precise connotation. It can be agreed that education is a process of change and that sometimes, at least, changes are mediated by an educator; but it is difficult to distinguish between spontaneous developments and those which are mediated. Moreover, all kinds of processes result in identifiable learning but in the absence of full information as to how learning proceeds and what are its results, it is hard to decide which of them merits an 'educational' label.

As contributions arrived it became evident that the subject was so large that it would justify a series of volumes to deal with different aspects of teaching and learning. At the present time (1968) four books are planned of which this, the first, examines objectives in higher education, relating them to techniques of evaluation and teaching methods. The coverage planned for the whole series is as follows :

1 Objectives in higher education

2 Students' learning and individual differences

3 Teaching methods

4 New techniques in teaching

but it must be stressed that this is a provisional list, since this General Introduction is being written at a time when the Working Party has by no means concluded the discussions. It will, however, serve to indicate the broad outlines of what is planned. Each book is composed of a set of papers, attributed to individual authors, who had all the normal responsibilities of their office. Contributions evolved towards their published form through a series of working drafts, which served as working papers into which criticisms and suggestions from the whole Working Party were integrated. Sometimes, as in Chapter 1 of the first volume, these contributions altered the nature of the original paper.

The priority of teaching objectives in the series does not only reflect an obvious logical sequence. Every member who has taken any continuing part in the group's discussions has come to hold the view that an adequate consideration of objectives is absolutely fundamental, that in its absence conclusions reached about methods, equipment and assessment may well be both superficial and sterile. This is important to note, since not all of them would have accepted this view when they joined the Working Party.

Finally, the whole Working Party wish to place on record their great appreciation of the help they have received from Elizabeth Bull, initially Secretary to the Research Unit on University Teaching Methods and more recently to the Department of Higher Education at the University of London Institute of Education. Without her continuous and most effective help with organizational and secretarial matters, it could not have functioned.

W.D. Furneaux

Professor of Education
Brunel University

November 1968

INTRODUCTION TO THE SECOND EDITION

The publication of this second edition of Objectives in higher education provides an opportunity for describing briefly the way in which the work of the Working Party on Teaching Methods has developed.

Members of SRHE and readers of its monographs will appreciate that the aims of the original Working Party were only partly realized by the production of the first edition of this volume and the two subsequent publications Aims and techniques of group teaching by Dr M.L.J. Abercrombie (of which a third edition will soon be appearing) and Technical aids to teaching in higher education by Mr Colin Flood Page.

Over the years the Working Party has changed its composition and under a new Chairman is now engaged in examining two more areas where the publication of monographs may be possible, Project Methods and the Role of the Teacher. Work is well advanced on the 'Projects' study and it is planned to follow this with a supplementary series of case studies.

Prior to the production of the further volumes, the second edition of Objectives in higher education brings up to date our thinking about the role of objectives in planning courses and curricula and draws attention to new materials which have become available.

This introduction also provides the opportunity of expressing the Society's gratitude to Professor Furneaux for the enthusiasm he showed and the encouragement he gave, as founder Chairman, to the original members of the Working Group in its formative years.

D.E.P. Jenkins

Director of General Studies
The City University

November 1973

MEMBERS OF WORKING PARTY ON TEACHING METHODS IN HIGHER EDUCATION (1968)

W.D. FURNEAUX, Professor of Education, Brunel University (Chairman)

M.L.J. ABERCROMBIE, Reader in Architectural Education, School of Environmental Studies, University College, London

Ruth M. BEARD, Professor of Educational Studies, Postgraduate School of Studies in Research in Education, University of Bradford

C.M. FLOOD PAGE, Lecturer, Postgraduate School of Studies in Research in Education, University of Bradford

J. FREEMAN, Research Fellow, Departmentof General Practice, University of Manchester

J.R. HARTLEY, Reader, School of Education, University of Leeds

F.G. HEALEY, Head of Department of Linguistics and Regional Studies, University of Surrey

P.J. HOLLOWAY, Reader in Community Dentistry, University of Manchester

D.E.P. JENKINS, Director of General Studies, City University

W.T. KOC, Research Fellow, Department of Psychology, University of Strathclyde

H.F. LUNN, Senior Lecturer in Physiology, Guy's Hospital Medical School

J. McLEISH, Professor of Educational Psychology, University of Alberta

H. WALTON, Professor of Psychiatry, University of Edinburgh

CONTENTS

ACKNOWLEDGEMENTS

I would like to thank all members of the Working Party who offered detailed criticism of successive scripts, especially Professor W. D. Furneaux and Dr F. G. Healey, and also members of staff in my own department and other readers who made helpful suggestions and criticisms. In particular, I owe thanks to Miss Elizabeth Bull and Miss Kay Pole, Secretary and Research Officer respectively in the Department of Higher Education, University of London Institute of Education and to Mr C. E. Gimson and a colleague of his in the Department of Electrical Engineering, University College, London for their comments on Chapters 1, 3 and 4, and to Professor L. Perry of the University of Warwick, who read and commented on the first draft of Chapter 3. I am also very grateful to Miss Bull and to Miss Angela Harley for their help in typing the successive, increasingly lengthy, typescripts of edition 1 and to Miss Gwen Heath and her colleagues for typing additional sections for edition 2.

Thanks are also due to the numerous people who allowed us to use material from their articles, books and courses. Without these illustrative examples our text would have been considerably less interesting and instructive.

RMB

We wish to thank all those whose assistance and helpful comments and criticism have guided us in the writing of Chapter 2. In particular, our thanks are due to Dr Ruth Beard, Miss Kay Pole and Professor W. D. Furneaux for their help in editing the final draft, as well as to all members of the Working Party for their comments at all stages of progress.

FGH
PJH

Chapter 1 | CHANGING OBJECTIVES IN HIGHER EDUCATION | Ruth M. Beard

Section I: CURRENT APPROACHES TO ANALYSIS OF OBJECTIVES

Introduction

Until the second half of the twentieth century, aims of education were a matter for discussion amongst philosophers, teachers and administrators. It was not until the 1950's, when programmed texts were first introduced and the methods of occupational psychologists began to be applied to classroom teaching and learning, that some psychologists entered the field. Their role, however, is of a different kind from that of the philosophers. They do not attempt to discuss values, except perhaps in the teaching of psychology, but play an advisory role to the teachers who are, themselves, responsible for the content of the course. The role of the 'educational technologist' who uses these new approaches is often to ask questions and to draw attention to factors which must be considered in course planning, in addition to giving assistance in clarifying ideas and in developing a systematic scheme.

Less than twenty years later the influences of this group has grown substantially in America, where a variety of techniques has been developed for individual study, and to a lesser but significant extent in some European countries. The most notable instance in England is at the Open University where courses are planned by interdisciplinary teams which include an educational technologist. It is his responsibility to assist the team in clarifying its objectives, to co-ordinate contributions to course books and television programmes and to decide with the team members how each course will be evaluated. Educational technologists are also employed in an advisory capacity by some professional bodies and specialist departments in universities and colleges to assist in designing new courses or in developing better ways of presenting and evaluating existing ones. In some of the polytechnics, psychologists who have this orientation plan courses for the teachers and provide written guides to assist them in designing their courses systematically.

By no means every psychologist who is concerned with objectives and their achievement thinks of himself as an 'educational technologist'.

The term tends to be associated in America with psychologists whose aim is to 'shape behaviour' in the classroom as Skinner has done that of animals in the laboratory. In a minority of American schools and colleges, teachers have been provided with objectives together with prescribed methods to follow during periods of class teaching. Thus they have been wholly robbed of initiative in a manner almost unknown in England where teachers normally have complete responsibility for planning their own courses and lessons.

It is understandable therefore that the progress of the educational technology movement has sometimes been viewed with disfavour and that the method itself has been criticized. At the simplest level, what is claimed and contested is that it is usually possible to specify 'behavioural objectives' – ie. to state what students will be able to do at the end of a course of study which they could not do initially, and to test the effectiveness of each course in terms of the achievement of these objectives. This objection may depend in part on a misunderstanding. The great majority of educational technologists do not imagine for one moment that they can wholly prescribe how an original piece of work will be performed, nor do they exclude creative activities from the scheme of objectives on this account. In activities of this kind they are content to state general objectives. Specific objectives are written for activities which can be more exactly defined, such as learning a body of knowledge or acquiring a particular skill. They therefore engage in two fairly distinct activities. In the first of these, they develop a system of general long-term and intermediate objectives which – with related activities in teaching and learning and methods of evaluation – serve to outline the entire course. This may take the place of a syllabus. The second activity consists in defining specific short-term objectives for particular topics. It is these objectives which may be used as a guide by teachers in preparing a topic, or as the first step in designing a programmed text or some other carefully planned activity for individual study. The industrial design course and a scheme for an undergraduate physics course, described later in the chapter, involve only specification of general objectives; but the book produced at Aarhus, Denmark, for the teaching and learning of a course in medical physiology, states aims (or general objectives) and in addition lists specific objectives for each successive topic.

Even when this distinction has been made, some teachers (and especially teachers of arts subjects) maintain that it may be harmful, or pointless, to specify objectives at all. They argue, for instance, that the outcomes of learning at higher levels are too complex to be stated or assessed in the short term. They cite instances of students having different goals and abilities whose achievements as a result of the same learning experiences differ widely; or they point to instances where the objective may be the same for every student but the means by which it is attained differ considerably from one student to another.

They are therefore concerned lest an attempt to define objectives, and to design courses in any detail, will limit students' goals and even the means they may choose to achieve them. If the educational technologist counters that a scheme of general objectives need not restrict learning in these ways, some teachers reply that the most valuable experiences in their courses cannot be defined at all or that any general objectives they could state would be so vague as to be meaningless. Since the majority of these teachers not only choose activities and offer courses of study for their students but also set examination papers which enable them to grade each student's performance, there is no doubt that they seek to achieve some results in preference to others and have standards which enable them to make comparisons. What is contested is whether these standards can be made explicit in terms of objectives and, if they can be, whether the resulting scheme will serve any useful purpose.

Yet if teachers claim that specification of objectives is unnecessary or useless, educational technologists and like minded teachers may fairly point to failures of existing methods of setting up courses and curricula. How is it, for instance, that combined courses sometimes 'just deteriorate' from the honours standard they were intended to maintain? Why do some so-called integrated courses consist of unrelated sections taught by specialists having little or no knowledge of those parts of the course for which they are not directly responsible? Why do students who take combined courses often do worse than similarly qualified students who opt for single honours courses? Do teachers, perhaps, demand too much without realizing it because they have never carefully analysed what the combined courses entail? And it is reasonable to echo the concern felt by teachers in the last century about fragmentation of courses when course units are subdivided so that, in theory at least, an undergraduate might obtain a degree by studying between thirty-six and forty-eight short courses each comprising a quarter unit!

In addition to problems relating to design of new courses which – unlike those at the Open University, for instance – seem to have been set up with insufficient analysis of their purposes and content, there are perennial problems. In too many courses the examination system is still at variance with the teachers' avowed aims. Many teachers lament that 'students work only for examinations', failing to see that this may be a criticism of their own course and system of evaluation. If the achievement of every important objective in some way contributes to the final assessment, and if it is apparent how different kinds of activities contribute to the whole course, it is unlikely that students will neglect any aspect of it unless they are overworked or the teaching is poor.

A further important argument for clearer communication of course requirements is that in its absence students often become frustrated and inactive. Some medical students say that they ceased to work in their first clinical year not, as is commonly supposed, because they were exhausted after intensive swotting for the second MB, but simply because they did not know what they should do. No-one told them what to read, or whether to read, they did not know what they should observe and were uncertain of their role with respect to the patients; and any attempt to talk with patients or to assist in the wards seemed to antagonize the nursing staff. So widespread was this feeling that at the end of 1972 medical students organized their own conference in which they spent three days learning how to specify objectives. Eventually they hope that they will develop detailed course schemes to discuss with their teachers. Similar frustrations which courses do little to dispel, are reported by students from other specialties.

Since the majority of teachers inevitably seek to influence their students' behaviour, there seems to be a case for stating, so far as is possible, what it is which they hope their students will achieve. A syllabus which consists only of a list of topics tends to direct attention to what students should know about at the expense of abilities, sympathies and skills which they need to develop. Thus they may easily neglect some of the most important aims in higher education since these are never mentioned.

2 The influence of modern developments on objectives in higher education

A well-established trend in higher education is the development of broader courses which provide opportunity to specialize in one or two different directions, as in combined honours courses, or which give opportunity to students to reconsider the direction in which they specialize. As new subjects develop and well-established ones change in content, the need for a broader-based education inevitably increases; for example, medical and biological students increasingly need mathematics or physics and designers nowadays require a knowledge of statistics. There is, therefore, a growing need for flexibility in planning courses so that needs can be met as they arise rather than when an accumulation of problems and discontent makes some action inevitable. It is also necessary to provide professional men and women with a sufficiently broad base of knowledge to be able to adjust to new subject matter, or new subjects, throughout their careers. One of the most thorough-going attempts is in the Foundation Year and broadly-based degree courses at the University of Keele; but other universities are insisting that students should study groups of related subjects, so avoiding a too-narrow specialization and reducing difficulty in communicating with specialists from other fields.

In other areas of study, additional subjects have become necessary owing to a growing concern with social relevance: for instance, students of law increasingly study some sociology; student engineers undertake projects in which they become more aware of the interconnections of technical questions with social political and economic ones; whilst many medical schools have fairly recently established departments of epidemiology or social medicine in which the lives and problems of local people are studied. In a typical project chosen for this purpose in an engineering school, groups of third year students are asked to examine a social or economic question to which engineering techniques can usefully be applied (Beard 1967). An important secondary aim of this scheme is to provide an opportunity to organize and carry out a co-operative investigation of some complexity.

Topics which have so far proved most successful include:

a A large electrical firm is investigating the possibility of setting up manufacturing facilities in Trinidad (West Indies). Draw up a report recommending a suitable project.

b Examine the economics of providing a secure electrical supply in England and Wales.

c Recommend a suitable transport system for use between Central London and London Airport.

In an end-of-term inquiry, more than half of the students reported that they learned about the problem of co-ordination between bodies working on different aspects of the same problem, while more than a third pointed out additional benefits in learning the best ways of collecting and clarifying information and what made for more effective oral reporting in a group.

Recognition of the need to encourage flexibility and inventiveness in young people has led to revision of whole courses and, in particular, to the development of programmes of laboratory experiments which are genuine problems. In this way students learn how to ask leading questions, to consult books and journals, to set up their own experiments which they discuss with fellow students or tutors and, finally, to make a full report of their procedures and attempted solutions, failures and successes. Teachers find that involvement in planning experiments leads to greater enthusiasm and at the end of the course their students have learned the essentials of a scientific approach in a way that those who merely repeat well-known experiments may never do.

Even more radical changes may ensue from the current scarcity of posts for scientists. Inevitably courses must be reconsidered to see whether they offer adequate preparation to students who will have to adapt to existing professional opportunities in a variety of non-scientific fields and perhaps to unexpected changes in the future. An over-supply of architects has already led some architectual schools to offer a diversity of choices which enable students to fit themselves for other opportunities in industry.

Possibly one of the greatest advantages of all courses which employ projects or 'open-ended' experiments of the kind we have just described is that they cater for differences between students, since each individual can follow his own chosen procedures and may sometimes select his own projects. In courses of industrial design, students follow their own bent from early in the course, choosing projects in agricultural design, household design and so on. Where such a variety of projects is possible it is important that objectives of the courses should be specified in terms of the procedures and strategies students must learn, instead of in terms of content.

This kind of approach is carried to its logical extreme in an integrated course at Manchester which is designed to give insight into the role of science in relation to politics, economics, industry and philosophy, while offering a broad coverage of physics and chemistry with some engineering and computer programming (Jevons 1970). It is perhaps significant that graduates for the course prove highly marketable.

A growing need to prepare students to co-operate with specialists in other fields is also felt by architects who, in planning a new town, for example, must co-operate with local authorities, engineers or surveyors as well as colleagues, builders and clients; and by doctors in large town practices which employ personnel from a number of ancillary services. These requirements are reflected in experimental projects in some schools of architecture and in the experiences planned for trainees wishing to enter general practice. In almost all professions individuals are called on to co-operate to an increasing extent, perhaps by working in teams, or in communicating information to committees consisting of specialists in other fields who make different assumptions, employ different concepts, have somewhat different modes of thinking and unfamiliar biases. Moreover, the widespread uses of new techniques of communication, in particular television, emphasize the need for greater skill in oral reporting, or in discussion, in addition to acquisition of some general knowledge of other fields. It is, therefore, of some importance that communication skills should be fostered in the majority of university courses.

There is already a trend to specify objectives in these ways, for content changes so rapidly in many fields that grasp of principles, and of the methods of applying them to solve unfamiliar problems, are increasingly important.

It seems likely that these new approaches to teaching herald a revolution similar to that in many primary schools where learning by rote and drill in factual materials during class work have now largely given way to group and individual activities or projects. This alters the function of the teacher from that of the authority who dictates exactly what content shall be learned, and when, to a guide who plans activities and answers questions but leaves some initiative to the learner in acquiring the necessary skills. The latter tends to be a more difficult and demanding role but it is generally found more rewarding.

A brief summary of this kind suffices to show that there is a need for constant review of syllabuses and curricula. The more systematically they are planned, the easier it is to see how objectives should be modified and to determine whether different forms of education are needed. But a systematic plan has, in addition, the advantage that it is a form of communication between teachers from different departments and between teachers and students.

3 Systematic analysis of objectives in planning courses

The publication of books for use by students in the Foundation Course at the Open University in 1970 has helped to familiarize teachers in higher education with the practice of stating aims for entire courses and specifying objectives for particular topics. Some such guidance seems almost essential where students rarely meet their teachers; but it can improve communication between teachers and students in many departments where at present students must wait for a course to unfold before they can appreciate what its purposes are. It is true that there is a sense in which students cannot appreciate fully the purpose of a course until they have studied it, any more than a traveller can understand a country he has not lived in, but initially, each profits from guidance as to what to expect. The traveller can buy a map and a variety of guides for tourists which should enable him to make his way with a minimum of stress. But an average syllabus is less informative than this. It more closely resembles geography books at the end of the last century which listed towns, rivers, peninsulas and so on, but offered no insight into the development and organization of a country and into the customs of its people. What students seek in their studies is a kind of 'cognitive map' sufficient to give them a sense of direction and to enable them to co-operate intelligently in planning their own activities.

An informative guide of this kind also serves to dispel misconceptions on the part of students. At the Open University when the first students of science received their course books and notes, some wrote to their teachers to say that they had not read the introductory paragraphs about objectives, but if their teachers would tell them what to learn they would do so. Presumably they had come to believe that study of science involves no more than acquisition of information about the subject. The discussion this engendered served to put them on the right path or, conceivably, in some cases resulted in their withdrawal and selection of a course of study to which they were better suited. Perhaps the apathetic students one hears about so frequently from teachers in universities suffer from precisely this kind of failure in communication? For if students have false views or insufficient knowledge about the directions in which they should progress, their efforts prove unrewarding and they must wait for the teacher's next lecture to direct each limited advance.

Thus systematic analysis of courses can serve a variety of purposes. The essence of the method is to specify objectives of the course in terms of the behaviours students will develop or acquire, in relation to 'inputs' such as resources in manpower and materials, the media and modes of communication and the initial states of the students. A psychologist (or a team of psychologists in America) with the teachers who are responsible for the course, then attempt to arrange the objectives in an order best related both to the structure of the subject and to students' learning, eg. from concrete to abstract or from specific cases to generalizations, and so prepare an outline of the course exhibiting successive objectives. This serves as a 'syllabus' which is available both to staff and students. Finally, they decide how the desired behaviours will be recognized and how to evalute them. Thus it is not sufficient to say that the students will 'understand' the subject for this does not provide an exact description of their changed behaviour. Instead, we should specify that they shall be able to recognize certain phenomena, to translate statements and principles into other terms, act on them or apply them. Or we should expect them to learn to interpret data, to analyse it or to interpolate where there are gaps in a sequence or to go beyond what is given by predicting further results. Thus we demand that they should show awareness of applications, consequences, corollaries, etc. in accordance with the conditions described, or with those which they themselves have deduced. It should be appreciated that this kind of analysis does not necessarily lead to 'highly mechanized' courses depending on machines and computers nor even to detailed and closely prescribed course schemes. It can be equally helpful in developing an informative guide to courses in which objectives are achieved mainly through projects, experimental work or creative writing. A few examples illustrate the range of its application.

An analysis of an Industrial Design Course serves to show just how informative and flexible the resulting plan of action can be (Piper 1967). The psychologist and teachers planned their analysis in six steps. Ideally there would have been an initial study of the work of designers in order to determine objectives in teaching but, owing to lack of time and money, objectives were defined during discussions between practising designers and those in the school. Secondly, the objectives were specified in terms of behaviours the students would exhibit at different stages, eg. in identifying problems, four levels of behaviour were outlined for the successive years of the course. Relevant stages were also identified in the writing of reports and in making systematic solutions of problems, etc.

Thirdly, these achievements were broken down to see in what ways they could be attained. Fourthly, the psychologist and teachers decided what contributions could be made to the course by each discipline. Fifthly, they prepared a chart, showing the required performance in each discipline at different stages in the course, which served in lieu of a syllabus and timetable to staff and students alike. Finally, they estimated the time required for a class of students to match the stated criteria and arranged some latitude for repetition.

The resulting course is basically a series of projects. The timetable does not state what will be designed but it does state which particular criteria the student is to meet during his completion of that project. In this way it serves as a guide in planning courses of lectures, seminars and guided reading, so that students can be prepared for each project immediately before work begins on it.

A number of advantages are reported over traditionally conceived courses; both staff and students are more clear as to what the course is designed to achieve; it can be readily adapted in response to developments; the task of assessing students' progress becomes more meaningful for it is possible to devise objective measures of the degree to which performance criteria are being met. Since the timetable is not a list of lectures etc., and teaching methods can be kept flexible, all that is required is that a given performance should be attained in a given time, by any method which the member of staff considers most suitable.

In contrast, Objectives for a course in physiology for medical students (Naeraa 1972), prepared at Aarhus University, Denmark, at first sight

presents an outline of detailed objectives allowing little latitude for choice or for students' differences on entry. Long-term and specific objectives together with a representative sample of test questions or problems are outlined throughout nearly 130 pages of text.
Each topic is structured to include fairly detailed descriptions of the terminal behaviour expected of the student at the end of the course, ie. how he should be able to apply his knowledge. In addition the factual knowledge he should have acquired is specified. Diagnostic tests are set throughout the two semesters whilst the course – which includes lectures, laboratory and group work as well as individual activities – is in progress. Despite the detailed prescription, the objectives may be used mainly to alert students to the need to acquire basic knowledge and problem solving skills. A variety of opportunities for learning is provided and there is no compulsion to engage in any one of them. Students may learn in what way they please. In addition the course is designed spirally, covering the same ground at increasing depth three times, so allowing the best prepared and most able students to complete it in one semester instead of two.

A third example – a scheme of objectives with related methods in teaching, learning and evaluation in undergraduate physics – supplies an outline of the knowledge, abilities and attitudes the course is intended to instil but does not provide the detailed prescription which would be needed for directed forms of individual study (Pole 1973). It communicates very much more to students than do traditional syllabuses: it shows the different kinds of learning required, methods to be used in achieving them and the varied forms of evaluation to assess their accomplishment. Thus it should dispel at once any false notion as to the nature of the course and to the kinds of activity required of the students.

A somewhat different kind of example is provided by a book of objectives prepared by Stones and Anderson (1970) of educational psychology for student teachers. Initially these were collected from a large number of psychologists in Colleges and Departments of Education. The authors found it helpful to specify objectives in a number of areas, eg. The Psychology of Human Learning, The Psychology of Teaching Cognitive Skills, The Psychology of Teaching Motor Skills etc., at three different levels, including several types at each level. At their first level are objectives of the highest generality, whilst at the third level are objectives indicating specific behaviours. Type A objectives at any level involve complex problem solving or creative activity (Bloom's levels 5 and 6); type B objectives require less complex problem solving skills (Bloom's levels 3 and 4); type C objectives require principle learning or acquisition of facts and knowledge (Bloom's levels 1 and 2). Thus, any type A objective at level 1 depends on the prior achievement of the appropriate type B objective at the same level; and this, in turn, depends on the achievement of the level 1 type C objective, and so on for other levels.

Some physicists have demonstrated another effective use of operational research techniques by using network analysis to guide research students in designing a research project. The initial network shows the steps from specification of the problem in general terms to the report of results and indicates an approximate time scale. Subsequent networks take each step and break it down further into interrelated sequences of activities. This serves the purpose of guiding an inexperienced student in all the steps of his research, giving him warning where he will need to make preparation in advance and ensuring that he will not overlook any essential procedure. The authors find that a programme of this type 'enhances the efficiency of all those concerned with the project by avoiding unnecessary effort and making it possible to plan technical assistance. It permits a continous assessment of progress and should advance the time at which a student reaches the critical stage when he produces more ideas than are provided for him.' A consequence of setting out the research programme as illustrated in Figure 1 is to show the director of studies that there is a limited range of investigations that can be successfully completed by a student who has only three years in which to learn the techniques of research and then carry out an investigation. If the apparatus is complex, the experiments must be short and assured of a positive outcome. If the experimental information required is extensive, the apparatus should be ready and in working condition for the student. If the apparatus and experimental methods are relatively simple then more time may be spent in theoretical investigations (Williams and Wooding 1968).

Thus, like the designers, these physicists have found the value of a detailed outline of objectives in guiding both staff and students, in improving the students' performance and increasing the possibility of evaluating the action they take.

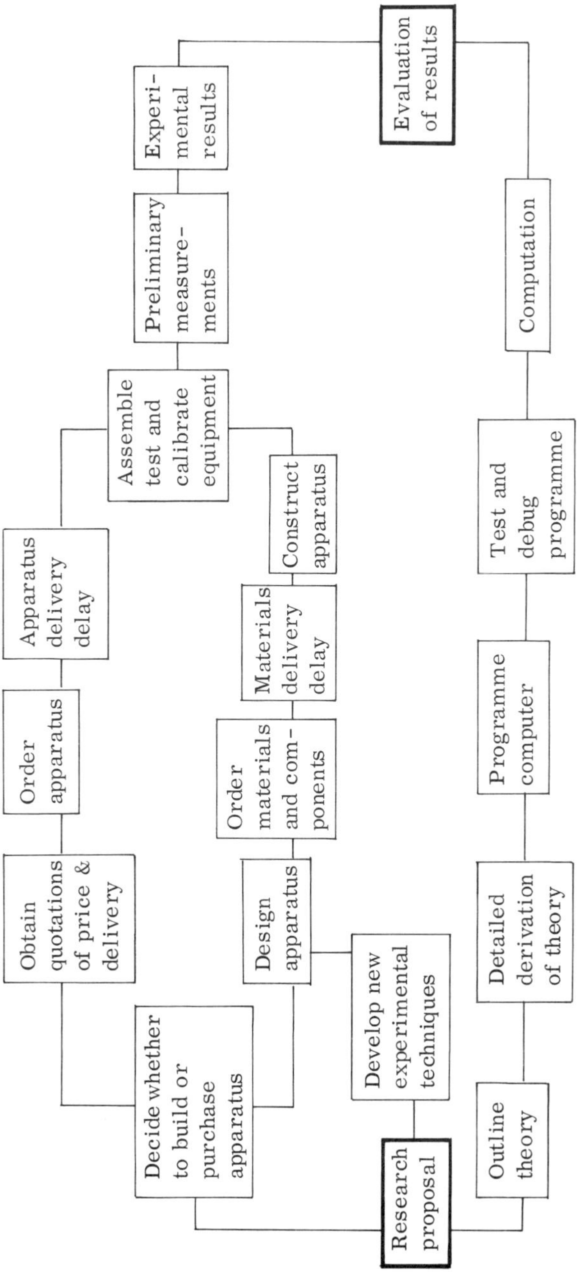

Figure 1 Stage 4 Experimental and theoretical investigation

4 A suggested procedure

During the last few years several books have become available in which methods of systematically planning courses are outlined. Somewhat different approaches are suggested in a UNESCO publication by MacKenzie, Eraut and Jones (1970) and in an unpublished Handbook prepared by David Baume and Brian Jones (1972) for use by teachers at North East London Polytechnic. Brian Lewis outlines methods employed at the Open University and discusses difficulties which inevitably arise in working with a team (1971 a and b, 1972). In each case, however, a number of stages are identifiable :

a As a preliminary to defining objectives and to preparing a systematic outline of a new course, Baume and Jones suggest that the teachers concerned should write down all the things which led them to decide that a new course was needed such as developments in the subject and related fields, students' views, conversations with colleagues, changing opportunities in employment, as these should suggest needs which existing courses fail to satisfy. In addition they should consider at this stage the probable length of the course, initial requirements of students and anything likely to affect the purpose and direction of the course, for instance opportunities for further study.

In the case of an existing course, if teachers decide to make explicit its objectives and their relation to methods in teaching and evaluation, Baume and Jones advise study of examination papers, statements which have been made about the aims of the course, model answers to examination questions and related syllabuses. These help to supply a list of activities which may be accepted as evidence that a student has attained an agreed level of performance under stated conditions. These activities, in their turn, serve as a basis from which to define objectives. As an illustration we will invent an example. Some teachers in science and engineering noting an increasingly close similarity in, say, physics and electrical engineering courses (or chemistry and chemical engineering) and feeling concern about reduced prospects of employment for pure scientists, propose to set up an integrated course. They suggest that this might produce a more flexible group of graduates who could seek employment in either field. A working party is set up to discuss the nature of such a course and requirements on entry.

b In the second stage a series of discussions takes place between the teachers concerned and the educational technologist or 'course-development consultant'.

The authors of the UNESCO publication favour the British practice of employing only one consultant, in preference to the multi-consultant advisory teams in America. They list its advantages as (i) it keeps the team reasonably small; (ii) the subject experts are dominant; (iii) it is economical in the use of consultant time; (iv) it develops consultants with wide experience; (v) the consultant is trained on the job.

In planning courses at the Open University, Lewis mentions 'several weeks of discussion on the aims, objectives and content of the course' before the academics go away to write their individual contributions. During this stage general, long-term objectives are stated and some intermediate objectives are specified. For instance in the case of our hypothetical integrated course, we might state in the first place:

At the end of the course students will

(i) have a knowledge of developments in pure science and of applications in engineering throughout the industrial world;

(ii) have a knowledge of concepts common to both fields;

(iii) be capable of solving problems in both fields;

(iv) be suitable for employment in either pure science or engineering, etc.

From this point, objectives will be specified in increasing detail and may extend to identifying individual steps in learning difficult topics as is the case in planning programmed texts.

c Following this outline of the course in terms of major objectives and of essential information skills and abilities, a series of objectives are set up for different stages in the course and only then is it essential to consider how each objective will be attained. The same outline may serve as a guide to highly individual courses in which each student proceeds at his own pace or planned courses in which teachers guide students at least in attaining initial skills. In either case the outline of objectives is made available both to staff and students, so enabling both to assess learning as it proceeds and motivating students by showing them what they have still to attain.

5 New audio-visual techniques and aims in teaching

The development of new techniques in itself challenges teachers to reconsider what they value most and thus wish to emphasize in teaching and learning. There is a danger that the prestige, or interest, in owning closed-circuit television or a room with teaching machines will influence judgment as to their value before it has been adequately investigated. Some university teachers, for example, hearing of the value of programmed learning, inquire about machines they should buy before investigating what programmes are available or considering whether the effort and cost of producing further programmes in a suitable form for the machine is worthwhile in their subject.

Closed-circuit television has considerable value in relaying materials to a far wider audience than would otherwise be possible and in showing those which are dangerous or inaccessible except to a camera. It is also time saving since materials from different sources can be co-ordinated and a variety of exhibits can be assembled on one occasion; thus time can be spared for discussion which would otherwise be occupied in travelling or in further lectures. Since records can be obtained fairly inexpensively on video tape, outstanding lectures may be kept for future audiences or recordings may be made to provide feedback to teachers and students as to their performance of some skill, eg. in giving a lecture or in making a physical examination of a patient. An accumulation of such records is valuable in illustrating good or poor techniques to other groups of students or for purposes of revision. Nevertheless, unless the apparatus is fairly fully used it may still be questionable whether it justifies the initial outlay and subsequent expenditure.

Techniques of almost universal value are those which can be used inexpensively to illustrate lectures or topics in group discussion or which can be adapted for individual study. Illustrations using the overhead projector, tapes and slides or film loops can be used in these ways. But in these cases the question is how can they be used most effectively? If used for individual study should illustrations be accompanied by questions for the student to attempt to reply to before he sees the correct answer? Or is it sufficient simply to accompany the illustrations by a continuous tape or script as is usually done?

Evidence from programmed learning suggests that the former is likely to be effective. If so, for successful presentation, the teacher who devises the audio-visual aid needs to outline his objectives, to break down the learning into steps and to consider the best order of presentation, number of illustrations and so on before he prepares the tests. Perhaps, ideally, he would prepare a number of alternatives and compare their effectiveness. In any case, he would need to determine what students learned by constructing suitable tests to administer before and after use of the individual study techniques, whether these are his own, prepared by other teachers, or commercially produced. For there is a potential danger in the commercial development of audio-visual aids, for example. The businessman's objective is necessarily profit, despite any concern he may have that his wares should be educationally useful; he is therefore likely to be satisfied with short-term success and may view with favour kinds of learning which lead to increased dependence on his wares whether this is in the long-term interests of the students or not.

Medical departments are making significant developments in the preparation of individual programmes using audio-visual aids. For instance, Engel at the BMA is collaborating with doctors and organizations in developing teaching books with visual aids and tests such as The management of cardiac arrest in hospital (Zorab et al. 1972) which enable a young doctor to work at his own pace through the subject, to see relevant illustrative material, to immediately test his prowess and, if necessary, to look up again any points of which he is uncertain. Some medical schools have also appointed educational technologists to develop individual teaching programmes in a number of medical subjects.

6 Developments in the economics of education

Parallel with social and professional pressures to modify educational programmes and techniques, there are increasing demands from those who pay for expanding higher education that it should be efficient. This raises interesting problems for economists and others who must first define concepts which will enable them to assess educational efficiency. Cost-effectiveness analysis is the most general tool, merely expressing the effectiveness with which objectives are achieved per unit of cost. If there is more than one, objectives may be appropriately weighted. This general technique is completely neutral about objectives, and although it has nothing to do with the content of economics, it is economists who naturally think like this. However, cost-effectiveness analysis is merely a formal way of stating the characteristics of all rational decision-making. Recent development includes introduction of 'programme budgeting' (Hartley 1968) which requires that 'outputs' or goals should be quantifiable to some extent so that projected expenditure data appearing in the budget can be meaningfully related to projected performance. This is in contrast to the conventional budget which is shaped largely by the desire to safeguard against carelessness and thus it does not allow resources and costs to be related to the specific 'outputs' or goals to be achieved. A key purpose of a 'programme budget' is to facilitate judgment about 'what is the least-cost method of undertaking a given activity'. However, as yet, 'output' measures appear to be somewhat crude.

The method of analysing and relating inputs and outputs known as 'systems analysis' is now in use at Toronto University in the Faculty of Medicine (Judy et al. 1968) employing objectives defined by teaching staff. A group of 'decision makers' then evaluate the costs and benefits of alternative programmes and so can answer 'What if....' questions as curricula and other changes are proposed. In this instance, the chief 'outputs' or objectives considered are education of health service personnel, patient care and research; the main categories of inputs are uneducated or partly educated students, academic and non-academic staff, facilities and materials and patients.

In the initial stage the purpose is to concentrate attention on the physical resources put into the system, but these are subsequently converted into monetary units.

The group of decision makers is now confronted with such problems as expansion of enrolment, increase in research, expansion of graduate studies, staffing and remuneration policy. To outline but one example of procedure given by the authors, once the total teaching load had been determined in terms of contact-hours between teachers and students, the effects of different staffing policies were considered in relation to estimated increasing of student numbers. Three staffing policies were considered:

A On the average six hours of teaching activity to be required per week per staff member;

B Staff members required to teach no more than two hours per week of lectures and seminars and no more than four hours per week of clinics, small groups and individual instruction whichever shall be limiting;

C Each department to require the same average number of teaching hours from its staff members as they provided in 1966-7.

It was shown that policy C necessitated significant increases in full-time staff (or their equivalents) above the levels forecast by departmental chairmen in their 1970/71 budget proposals except in Departments of Obstetrics and Gynaecology where the needs would decline by about one quarter; whereas policies A and B resulted in substantially lower requirements than those forecast, A requiring least.

The common assumption that, if the same objectives may be obtained by an additional member of staff, more space or an expensive piece of equipment, that the member of staff should be chosen, deserves to be examined with some care. One member of staff may be paid an average of £3,000 p.a. for 30 years, additional space may well cost about £10,000, whereas expensive apparatus, such as a language laboratory or closed-circuit television may require an initial outlay of only £4,000, although running costs and depreciation must be considered. If this is the situation, the teacher needs to be greatly superior in his effect on learning to justify so considerable a difference in expenditure.

The new budgeting is not an imminent development throughout the universities of Britain, but the interest aroused by the reports of Blaug (1968) and Blaug and Woodhall (1965) leaves us in no doubt that productivity and efficiency at all levels in education will soon be the subjects of similar inquiries. Although the indices used were experimental, their observation that measurement of productivity in British university teaching between 1938 and 1962 – employing three different weighting systems to evaluate the output of students completing a course – showed a steady decline by all three methods is disquieting, especially when they report the sharpest drop in the last ten years; but one way to contest their conclusions would be to demonstrate that they had neglected some important objectives in teaching.

In planning buildings for the future, flexible designs are being advocated to allow for different uses as subjects develop or teaching methods change; and the insistent demand that space and expensive apparatus in educational buildings should be used more fully is leading to consideration of laboratories in which more than one science can be taught. There are also proposals for a six-term year (Carter 1968) and for concentration of courses in a limited number of university buildings. In teaching, new techniques have been devised which allow some economy in the use of skilled teachers, such as extensive use of programmed learning (Romiszowski 1967, Wallis et al. 1966) or libraries of tapes and slides for use in private study by students and doctors at home and overseas or by those who lack access to teachers (Graves and Graves 1967). There is an increased concern also with evaluation of the effectiveness of learning and teaching. This requires careful analysis of objectives both to ensure that the information, skills and attitudes of greatest importance are taught and to avoid methods of examining which neglect certain attainments or give undue emphasis to those of less importance.

Section II: THE RELEVANCE OF LEARNING PROCESSES TO THE STUDY OF OBJECTIVES

1 Varieties of learning processes

The processes employed in teaching and learning are themselves relevant to a consideration of long-term objectives, for they reflect the values of teachers and influence the attitudes to learning of students as well as partly determining the kinds of skills and abilities they attain. We will discuss some processes relevant to the achievement of educational purposes beginning with those already apparent in infancy (which nevertheless continue and develop throughout life) and proceeding to those which involve the use of symbols and abstractions.

a Processes which are largely unconscious

The most primitive processes in learning include the development of schemas of perception and action, conditioning, suggestion, imitation and identification. These are processes which are to a considerable extent involuntary, making minimal use of language and which therefore dominate learning until the emergence of language causes their importance in a pure form gradually to decrease.

Perceptual schemas are built up in infancy from many observations of similar events. Thus, if we look at the photograph of a boiler of a ship and see a line of small circular shapes with shadows on their lower edges we interpret them as rivets; large irregular rounds with shadows in their upper segments may be interpreted as damage from gunfire. If we reverse the picture the rivets appear hollows and the 'indentations' are now protruberances (Abercrombie 1966). All our lives we have expected light to shine from above and so we interpret pictures accordingly. Again, an individual accustomed to rectangular buildings on looking into a distorted room in which floor, ceiling and walls are all trapezia is liable to interpret what he sees as a normal room in perspective (Kelley 1947).

Every individual has a multiplicity of such representative schemas of which he may be unconscious but without which he could not interpret the world he lives in. Physiologically their basis seems to be in the gradual organization through repeated experiences of patterns of cellular activity in the cortex, which operate as integrated wholes. These are activated whenever the individual experiences relevant stimuli. During infancy, schemas of action and perception are developed but, with the acquisition of language and ability to represent one thing by another, first representative schemas and then conceptual schemas are developed and these, in turn, are integrated into more complex organizations. The acquisition of perceptual schemas therefore is a kind of learning essential to subsequent education; but it proceeds at a level where the deliberate intervention of other individuals is unnecessary and the learner does not reflect on what he does. When in later life representative schemas are extended with the assistance of language, in learning the meaning of 'square' for example, or in interpreting diagrams and X-rays, the intervention of a teacher is practically unavoidable and the individual is aware that he learns – or that he fails to do so. Moreover, the learning process is a more complex one. It may be, however, that the kind of representative schemas developed unconsciously in infancy, whether predominately visual or auditory and kinaesthetic, determine the directions of later learning and the choice of educational specialities. This is sometimes described as an unconscious co-ordination of mental schemas of action which operate in learning a skill by imitation; it is possible to develop a 'feel' for the chain of actions which constitute the skill before performing them, although of course performance is essential to expertise. Imitation is, therefore, a useful process which the learner is conscious of employing; but some imitation takes place at a less conscious level where, for example, a slow worker is influenced to work more rapidly in the company of a highly practised or quicker group.

Identification appears to be more wholesale imitation of an individual having prestige or the taking over of behaviour characteristics of a group. Among students it may be at least partly a conscious process of modelling behaviour on an admired teacher or, in schools, pupils may model themselves on an older pupil. It appears that this process is used in schools which foster an ideal type, and that it is one factor in operation when a student doctor, for example, acquires professional attitudes.

Conditioning is an automatic association having direct consequences on behaviour which associationists claim to use in teaching. In classical conditioning first studied by Pavlov, an association is set up between a neutral stimulus (such as the ringing of a bell) and a reflex action (such as salivating on the presentation of food). This results, after several simultaneous presentations, in the neutral stimulus being followed by the reflex reaction without the presentation of the present stimulus, ie. the sound of the bell alone results in salivation. In instrumental conditioning an action of the animal (or human being) is instrumental in producing a 'reward' of some kind; in consequence the probability of the action being repeated is enhanced. For example, if pressing a lever more or less accidentally produces food this leads to an animal eventually 'learning' to press the lever. This 'learning' may then be utilized in a different situation. In both kinds of conditioning therefore, reinforcement by a 'reward' of some kind results in the setting up of patterns of behaviour. In the case of programmed learning, the learner is rewarded by the satisfaction of knowing that he has made the correct response to the stimulus which takes the form of a written statement or question; thus he learns by instrumental conditioning.

The processes of imitation and identification, like suggestion, have in common that they all play an important part in learning, which usually requires human contact, but it is a part which tends to decrease with age and maturity in the learner. Some types of suggestibility appear to depend on the use of language for they develop after infancy to a maximum at about eight years but thereafter decline as capacity for critical thinking develops. However, individuals differ in the extent to which their behaviour and mental processes can be influenced without their knowledge and volition, and susceptibility varies also with the situation or with the kind of personal interaction. Although people are likely to be suggestible in relation to others with prestige this is not necessarily the case. There is some evidence that, in relation to prestige figures, people rarely make luke-warm responses; they are either strongly influenced in favour or against their views or quite uninfluenced by them. Whereas, in situations where prestige plays no part, most people are somewhat suggestible. Interestingly, suggestion which is usually verbal and spoken may be equally effective when recorded (Hull 1933).

In the case of 'indirect suggestion', where the response is suggested in such a way that individuals are unaware of being directed to behave in a particular manner, up to 90 per cent of experimental subjects prove susceptible (Hull 1933). When samples of students were asked to read a passage, either silently or aloud, or to prepare a talk on the same topic, those who prepared and delivered a talk were significantly more influenced by the passage than those who did not (King and Irving 1956). This raises questions about whether teachers may not suggest the acceptance of certain views merely by asking students to report on them, or to be otherwise involved in defending them, and stresses the need - where rational thinking is the objective - for presenting several views (if these exist) at one time. Perhaps the experiment 'succeeds' by the same mechanism as one used by Festinger and Maccoby (1964) who distracted their audience while a message unwelcome to some of them was put over. They showed a persuasive film arguing strongly against fraternities, once with and once without the addition of highly distracting material. Results indicated that those who had no strong views were not influenced by either presentation but that those previously committed in favour of fraternities were influenced by the film with distracting material, but not by the other, presumably because the distracting material prevented them from formulating counter arguments.

The importance of being able to formulate and present a contrary view in resisting suggestion is supported by findings which show that those who initially asserted their independence in face of views they found unpalatable tended to remain uninfluenced (Gerard 1964), and by a study where an inverse relationship was found between suggestibility and conscious, verbalizable resistance to test suggestions (Barber and Calverley 1963). In an experiment by Lorge (1936) students did not, in general, base their judgments about the validity of statements on the prestige of the writers to whom they were attributed, but considered the whole context for the determination of meaning.

In group situations among students Asch has reported a 'predisposition to conform' (1956); but independence of judgment had been established by about half the groups studied. He showed also that where standards of a congenial group differed sharply from those of an individual member, his standards were weakened as a basis for judgment whereas those of an antagonistic group tended to be rejected – and more decisively so in contrast with that of the congenial group than in comparison with the ego-standard; individuals whose views differed considerably from those of the congenial group were more likely to change than those who diverged slightly (Asch 1940, 1948, 1956).

A characteristic common to all of these learning processes is that each may have an effect either of directing or limiting learning – an individual's belief in his capacity to succeed may be undermined by indirect suggestion, he may imitate undisciplined behaviour from companions in a group or, in childhood, he may have identified with an immature or delinquent parent or companion and, through conditioning, he may acquire stereotyped responses. Suggestion is also one of the tools in deliberate indoctrination. Since such learning is non-verbal it is relatively inaccessible to persuasion and still less to reasoning. Experimental results show that the chief defence, or remedy, is that students should develop the capacity to express resistance in verbal form. To aid this process teachers should encourage discussion of a variety of viewpoints and help students to become more critical by being aware of their own assumptions and prejudices. In so far as more primitive learning processes are used, their function in higher education appears to be to foster confidence, to motivate students to learn or to induce desirable professional attitudes; and, since group influences are bound to operate, the composition of groups in teaching would be likely to repay study.

b Processes which are conscious but automatic

A second group of learning processes is less automatic and depends to some extent on deliberate teaching. These are rote learning, following rules, training or practice which give rise to acquisition of information or skills, and –of a somewhat different nature since it may employ any of the former processes – indoctrination. A feature of all these kinds of learning is that they are limited as educational processes; the student knows something or is able to do something without knowing how, or he believes something without reason or despite information which should cause him to reconsider his belief. However, each one has a place in education; rote learning is useful in acquiring vocabulary and the alphabet, for example, and a few people excel in learning this way; following rules is essential in circumstances when the learner must act but has insufficient knowledge to exercise judgment; practice is needed to learn arithmetical combinations and indoctrination of a kind is inevitable when children are introduced to beliefs which they are too immature to question. The value of these processes is in doubt if they continue despite the pupil's growing ability to be more critical or to learn general principles, or if they are substituted for those kinds of learning which lead to understanding of concepts, discriminations, techniques in problem solving, and so on.

c Learning processes which maximize understanding

The learning processes which remain are those which maximize understanding, require the pupil to act independently and to make decisions, demand flexibility in thinking or some inventive or creative effort. It is the developments arising from these processes which are increasingly required as knowledge develops ever more rapidly. Yet it is precisely at this level of complexity that there has been insufficient analysis of learning for us to pinpoint the processes involved. However, we will attempt to identify broad categories which involve fairly independent activities.

A process which begins in early life and continues as long as intellectual growth continues is that of asking and answering questions. From this develops the give and take of conversation and of more organized discussion. There is evidence that this is one of the most educative processes since it enables the pupil to analyse differences in views and opinions, revising his position to integrate what he learns with what he already knows. Berlyne found that to ask questions, particularly unexpected ones, rather than stating facts, improved learning and increased interest in a topic (Berlyne 1954). Students must learn special skills in asking questions whether they are to become scientists who plan experiments, lawyers who will try to arrive at the truth about events or social workers or doctors who must attempt to diagnose the sources of their patients' problems or illnesses. Discussion in adolescence and adult life also contributes to the development of new concepts from already familiar ones or from those imperfectly understood in reading.

Solving problems is another process which is learned early in life; but successive problems once solved become familiar facts. In childhood, problems are largely of a kind which lead to concept formation –

to recognition of ways of categorizing objects or to establishing relationships between them. In adolescence, and throughout higher education, although concepts are learned, they tend to be more abstract in nature and the greater part of problem solving involves the application of known principles and the derivation of more complex and general ones. At a still higher level, the principles may be interrelated in explanations or in theories in an attempt to solve yet more complex or fundamental problems.

A third process which develops throughout life is that of decision-making. In this aspect, perhaps, traditional education is weak – for children's decisions are mostly made in play and are, therefore, outside the organized educational process. It is, of course, one of the virtues of the modified Dalton Plan (Parkhurst 1930) that children decide for themselves during a large part of the day what they will study, selecting from books suggested in the syllabuses provided by their teachers and with latitude as to when to complete homework. No pupils of these schools suffer the problem of not knowing how to organize their studies on arrival at university. But this is only one example of decision making, albeit an important one. Pupils make decisions whenever they work independently in planning experiments or in producing a play, for example, or whenever they are given responsibility; and, to a lesser extent, they learn by seeing how decisions are made by other people. However, as with all skills, ability to make good decisions is learned by practice and feedback as to success.

In every subject there are many skills and abilities which require practice such as writing of reports, learning points of grammar, acquiring skill in speaking a language or solution of particular kinds of mathematical problems. There is no substitute for practice with prompt correction of errors or reinforcement of correct responses. However, where teaching is poor, practice of this kind tends to occupy a disproportionate amount of time to the exclusion of the solution of learning processes which encourage greater activity and understanding on the part of the student.

Processes which contribute to personality development, to skill in communication and to intellectual appreciation are those of externalizing experiences in terms of active expression. In these cases, if technical skills are not practised, the expression attained is likely to be inexpert; but it is in trying to convey an experience, emotion or idea that the artist or writer extends his repertorie of skills and may attain a more complete understanding in criticizing his own partial realization of it.

In addition to self-expression, the processes of analysis and evaluation are used to increase understanding of construction in the arts or presentation of scientific data or theories. These are skills appropriate on the whole to at least an adolescent level of attainment for they involve appreciation of relationships within a complexity which as we shall see, is not normally achieved until a mental age of 16 or so is attained.

2 Social influences on learning processes

We have considered educational processes at some length because it seems to us that although certain 'primitive' processes inevitably operate in education they tend to be ignored, and because different emphases on the completely rational processes, or the less rational, are associated with the beliefs and values of different societies and sub-groups. All advanced industrial societies have common objectives in attainment of the knowledge and skills required in management, scientific and technological development or communication, and have a substantially common heritage in the arts, and to this extent, must have very similar educational programmes and employ closely similar educational processes. Thus all these societies have many common goals, as well as common problems. It is at the ideological level that they differ substantially and it is in promotion of ideologies and group beliefs that the processes of suggestion, direct or indirect, and indoctrination are commonly used. Thus, in certain communities a young man may be educated as a scientist to criticize evidence, but in the social and religious fields he will not be trained to consider all the evidence, or it may not be available to him. This is highly criticized by those who feel free to study any view; but in so doing, they are accepting a value which is not self-evident and needs to be justified on other grounds. Also within a single society different institutions reflect different beliefs and, therefore, employ different processes in educating students. The contrast between the tutorial systems at Oxbridge and Sussex (when they result in genuine discussion) and the relatively slight contact between staff and students in some civic universities reflects one such difference in view.

In times of change there is a danger that learning processes suited to a past stage in development will continue to be employed when they are unsuitable or detrimental or they may be swept away on entirely inadequate grounds. It seems that this is so in some departments and in some areas of higher education; there is a habitual emphasis on rote learning, practice of known problems, experiments or skills although these may soon be outdated - and too little encouragement to students to think, to devise their own experiments or to attack genuine problems. Students complain that too many teachers maintain a consistently authoritarian attitude and thus fail to encourage them to be independent or to take responsibility for their progress. At all these levels we need to reconsider objectives in higher education and how we should employ the means available to us to produce professions competent to operate in the industrial society of the future where developments will accelerate with ever greater rapidity.

Since some new programmes are criticized by a number of university teachers for emphasizing a change in attitudes towards scientific investigation, whilst encouraging school children and students to give inadequate attention to acquiring a rigorously examined body of knowledge, experimental evaluation of alternative programmes might be the most rational way to decide on their respective merits.

Section III: OBJECTIVES IN HIGHER EDUCATION

Objectives in providing higher education are necessarily largely determined by the society it caters for. In communities where only some people receive formal education, or where an élite receives a superior education, its purpose is to prepare them to be responsible both for government and the advancement of knowledge. In Britain, until after the First World War, this was an education based on the classics in conformity with existing social ideals; the 'educated man' was, therefore, almost synonymous with the product of Oxbridge. Today, when everyone receives at least ten years of formal education, higher education follows both on social advantage and on evidence that the individual has capacity for higher intellectual attainments, and a man may be considered educated though he has no knowledge of the classics. The present purposes of higher education are to produce individuals, expert in various specialities, to maintain and develop the economy and to advance knowledge in an increasing number of fields. But as the number of specialized fields increases so does the importance of communication and this may lead to problems if higher education is not sufficiently broadly based. These are likely to be particularly acute in Britain where specialization begins in the schools and is more complete than in any other industrial country.

Perhaps some reassurance may be gained from the increasing number of interdisciplinary courses. As an instance, a course which five years ago was for senior architects from developing countries, now accepts specialists of all kinds concerned with the planning of the environment, eg. architects, administrators, planners, surveyors, economists. The teaching staff on the course has been diversified in the past five years from architects exclusively to specialists drawn from almost as many specialties as the course members themselves.

1 Common educational attainments

That there are nevertheless certain general higher educational attainments was shown by the empirical investigations of Piaget and Inhelder and despite early specialization these have been confirmed in Britain (Mealings 1963, Peel 1966). They found that the educated adolescent (with mental age of some 16 years or so) attained a number of characteristics in his thinking which were superior to those of children.

The process starts – and Piaget believes that this may be essential to the other developments – when the adolescent begins to see himself in relation to other persons and to appreciate the validity of their different views; he therefore becomes capable of making objective judgments and it is a short step to making assumptions and to deriving their consequences as he needs to do in science and in logical argument. This, therefore, is a capacity which resembles Peters' 'respect for others' (Peters 1966); but the latter is based on a concern for other people in addition to the intellectual component of simply seeing that other views exist than the individual's own. Thus, if Piaget is right that this capacity precedes other higher developments in thinking, it must be only the intellectual component that is essential, for some who lack concern do achieve intellectual eminence, and history would be deprived of its autocrats and selfish manipulators of other men if respect for others had been a condition for intellectual superiority.

Secondly, the educated adolescent seeks general laws and principles; for example, he finds common meanings to proverbs and understands some more complex principles in science and mathematics. However, observation suggests that at the university less able students often cannot select appropriate principles or generate new ones whereas the honours student may excel in these respects. Thus, in teaching at this level, one objective may more properly be to enable students to select from a repertoire of principles in solving or discussing varieties of problems than merely to apply known principles to problems of stated kinds.

Thirdly, the educated adolescent takes a broader view than a child; he considers different aspects of a case, gives exhaustive definitions and no longer makes moral judgments in black and white terms. Failure to develop in this respect may be one reason why some students give descriptive answers to questions they are required to discuss. It is possible that concentration on physical sciences and mathematics encourages students to look for the one right approach or one correct answer (at least as these subjects are frequently taught). One of the writer's students who had a third-class degree in mathematics, but many practical interests, observed that he was not in the habit of looking at different sides of a question. He had been puzzled when a descriptive answer to a question he was required to discuss had received a poor mark, but he realized suddently that he had this particular deficiency. This instance suggests that a too narrow specialization, or a too narrow approach in teaching, may limit capacity for higher attainments in thinking.

Fourthly, adolescents learn to use some complex relationships such as proportionality, correlation and probability, or relationships within a complexity when sifting data, in planning experiments or following events in history. In addition, capacities specific to certain fields are attained: eg. in solving problems of a scientific nature the adolescent at this level sees the need to alter one variable at a time, sets up his own experiments and tests hypotheses he makes, thus developing an increasing capacity to organize his thinking and to argue deductively.

Overall the thinking of the adolescent is more abstract than that of the child. He thinks in verbal and symbolic terms, arguing in propositions, and goes beyond the concrete, tangible and finite to deal with the intangible, infinite or imaginary. His behaviour becomes increasingly guided by principles which he has thought through. Nevertheless, findings in a study of understanding of television programmes (Treneman 1967) show that even highly intelligence and well-educated adults understand better a concrete, rather than an abstract, approach. Thus, in teaching new topics even at university level, an initial approach through concrete examples is likely to facilitate later understanding of abstractions.

Moreover, comments by university teachers suggest that development of thinking is not completed by the age of 16 years but that a further development, for instance in handling evidence, takes place in late adolescence and early adult life.

2 Individual differences and objectives

Since Piaget and Inhelder did not investigate the thinking of adolescents older than 16 years they had no opportunity to trace the development of ways of thinking specific to certain domains or to study highly original and complex thinking in young adults. For example, no one has studied the effect of specializing in one field on thinking in others; but the tendency to fail to comprehend each other observed among some specialists, eg. some surgeons and psychiatrists, or physical scientists and social scientists, suggests that a highly specialized education may limit ability to communicate with people from other fields or alternatively that a personality factor operates in the original choice of speciality and simultaneously causes antipathy to extremely different ones. A number of philosophers claim to have distinguished between different domains of knowledge in terms of different bodies of concepts and modes of thinking. Initially, Peterson (1960) listed the lyrical, empirical, moral and aesthetic as the main modes of thinking. Hirst (1967) suggests that the distinct disciplines or forms of knowledge are mathematics, physical science, human sciences and history, religion, literature, the fine arts and philosophy together with moral knowledge and that these at the present time basically constitute the range of unique ways we have of understanding experience. Historically, he considers, there has been a progressive differentiation, the most recent division being between religion and morals, but as bodies of concepts are developed in new fields additional domains of knowledge are likely to evolve.

Broad differences in ways of thinking between specialists in sciences and arts or social sciences, have been found in English sixth formers by Hudson (1966) who identified them as 'convergent' and 'divergent' thinkers. Their characteristics were reported as follows: 'the converger enjoys thinking about technical, impersonal matters. He likes argument to be clearly defined and logical, and to know when he is right and when wrong. He is not interested in probing into topics of a personal, emotional nature, nor in controversy. The diverger is the reverse, he likes discussion to be personal, he enjoys controversy and uncertainty. On the other hand, he is not interested in the technical, nor in argument which is purely a matter of impersonal logic'. The former type tends to elect to study the physical sciences whereas divergers more often choose the arts or social sciences. People who make decisions based on probabilities before it is clear whether their decisions are good ones may tend to be divergers.

To what extent these differences are educationally determined is difficult to say. Possibly they are determined more by early upbringing or even by innate differences. But, since most differences between individuals are modifiable by education, we should infer that a broadly based education will serve to reduce the number of extreme convergers and divergers, whereas their number will be greater among students who had specialized very early in arts or sciences. When specialization takes place, as it must in many courses, the necessary emphasis on certain kinds of concepts, modes of communication and expression, and criteria for distinguishing true from false, or good from bad, almost inevitably lead to biases in thinking. However, it will be interesting to see whether broader based courses, such as the Foundation Year at Keele, result in a greater ability even on the part of average students to communicate with those in other fields.

Individual differences in perceptual type possibly of a fundamental kind, since they are related to wave patterns of brain activity, have been demonstrated by Grey Walter (1961). In 1943 he found that individuals with persistent alpha rhythms, which were hard to block with mental effort, tended to auditory, kinaesthetic, or tactile perceptions rather than visual ones. In this group alpha rhythms continued even when their eyes were open and their minds were active or alert. A second group, who showed no alpha rhythms, conducted their thinking processes almost entirely in visual terms; whereas the remainder of the sample, whose alpha rhythms began when their eyes were closed and their minds relatively inactive, employed all modes of perception more easily. The proportion of individuals using visual perception almost exclusively proved somewhat higher in science students than among those specializing in arts; they were quick in solving problems which could be readily visualized but when faced with an abstract problem or ones which they found too complex to visualize adequately, they became 'sluggish and confused'. Since the majority of children are visualizers it will be of interest to know what are the results of experiments in which the development of thinking and perception as well as alpha activity is followed with a view to determining to what extent these also are influenced by experience.

Other factors which may well influence choice of speciality and of biases in thinking are such special cognitive abilities as speed and skill in calculating, verbal fluency, spatial imagination, verbal and non-verbal reasoning, perceptual speed and so on, which some psychologists identified in the 1930's and 1940's (Vernon 1961). Personality factors such as introversion-extraversion must also lead to educational choices which eventually, if not initially, are associated with different modes of thinking.

Since individual differences are so great, there seems to be a case for greater flexibility in courses and in teaching. There is already a movement in this direction in the development of new kinds of combined courses and by allowing students to select subjects for projects and researches or to solve open-ended experiments; but there are still too many institutions where all students are expected to attend identical courses, to learn in the same way and to work at the same pace. In addition, a diversity of courses seems advisable when change is so rapid that it is impossible to predict what combinations will be most favourable in 10 or twenty years time.

3 Varieties of higher education

Findings relating to the development of thinking, and of different varieties of thinking in adolescents, or among kinds of specialists, enable us to consider objectives in higher education in a more informed way. In the second chapter, nineteenth-century views are discussed, in particular those advocating education in the liberal arts and the utilitarian view. The former was an education for the gentleman who did not require to earn a living, whereas, in contrast, the utilitarian reflected the attitudes of the rising industrialists and stressed the value of education in mastering the environment and advancing technological progress. Today a purely 'utilitarian' view, as such, is rarely expressed; instead vocational training is more likely to be contrasted with an enriched conception of a liberal education. For example, Peters (1966) suggests three conditions which a higher education should satisfy in order to be 'liberal': study of the subject matter should be worthwhile in itself, there should be an emphasis on rational thinking, judgment and criticism and it should not be restricted to a specialist training or to one mode of thought.

To many young people and to some of their elders this may seem to place too great an emphasis on rational aspects of learning. They may well wish to extend the concept of a liberal education to include development of an active concern for the welfare of other human beings.

Criticism of some postgraduate education derives from its failure even to meet the three criteria proposed by Peters. Some research topics are so narrowly conceived that their sole value may be in use of research techniques; whilst scientists who join a research team may have so limited a role that there is almost no opportunity to exercise judgment and little, if any, need to employ varied modes of thinking.

In discussing higher vocational education, Oakeshott (1962), observes that pursuit of the pure sciences and arts differs from vocational education because the former is an education in 'language', ie. it requires a thorough grasp of concepts and principles and a certain facility in using them, together with an appreciation of the internal standards of the subject and of its methods of inquiry and criteria of validation. Vocational subjects, on the other hand, resemble a study of 'literature'; that is to say, they require only a sufficient grasp of the subject matter for appreciation of substantive assertions in the texts and a modest acquaintance with the concepts and principles.* Thus university studies of a non-vocational kind may provide a 'liberal education' for they satisfy two of the three conditions given by Peters. However, the third condition is not necessarily satisfied, but depends on the breadth of the course in the university, or previous courses, and on teaching which emphasizes general principles and their application. It is clear, however, that such vocational studies as medicine, education or management studies which employ knowledge from the 'pure' disciplines may by these definitions provide a liberal education given that the command of the 'languages' of the various disciplines is at a sufficiently high

---

* Teachers of literature may feel that this is a poor use of the word. He would have done better to compare vocational education and an ability in translation which may proceed without a sound knowledge of language and still less requires the knowledge of human experience on which literature is based.

level to allow further learning and flexibility as knowledge develops. That is to say, there are higher vocational studies which, like applied sciences, may be a form of liberal education (Wall 1967).

However, as subjects change and merge, so that almost everyone in the professions needs to be able to accept ideas from other disciplines or to understand arguments based on the 'languages' of other domains, the need for a broadly based education increases. Moreover, it may be worthwhile to consider studies of topics and ways of thinking which have wide application - for example, the study of probability with its application in the physical and human sciences, industry and design and in problems which arise in making decisions in contexts such as medicine, politics, engineering or industry. Industrialists commonly assert that some kinds of specialized education tend to foster a desire for certainty; for example, they report that among graduates in physical sciences who choose to go into industry to train as managers, some are at a loss to make decisions when not all the information is available to enable them to arrive at a uniquely best solution.

The biases which we have observed in the thinking of specialists in different fields no doubt account for the different conceptions of higher education which are advocated today. Peters (1966), for example, criticizes Lord Bowden's view that higher education should devote itself 'like MIT and Caltec, to providing the theory necessary for solving the practical problems of the community'. Perhaps it is an opposite bias which leads philosophers to wish to extend the life of the concept of 'liberal education' – a concept which originated when education in the sciences hardly existed – rather than to develop a new, more comprehensive concept appropriate to the development of wider fields of knowledge and different attitudes occasioned by the growth of the human sciences. To speak of education as initiation into 'the skill and partnership of conversation' is partly true – and may seem entirely so to the philosopher with an arts bacground – but it neglects those aspects of higher education which give rise to activity not only in improving men's thinking but also in modifying their environment to gain increasing control of it. Perhaps we might speak of a 'humanitarian' education or employ the combined terms 'liberal and humanitarian' where we have in mind that those who profit from higher education should not only develop their own capacities for rational thinking in a number of domains of knowledge but also feel such concern for the welfare of their fellows that they apply their increased understanding to the benefit of humanity.

Chapter 2 THE 'CLASSICAL' OBJECTIVES OF UNIVERSITY TEACHING

F.G. Healey and P.J. Holloway

The use of the term 'objective' is probably less familiar to the majority of teachers in higher education, at least as a term of art, than is the expression 'the aim of education'. This has been widely used by the theorists of higher education to denote long-term objectives, the achievement of which, through some specific educational process or experience, typifies the successful product. In passing it is worthy of note that the possibility of success not being achieved by a favoured method or type of institution is a factor hardly ever taken into account by most of the theorists. Objectives may be of various kinds – short-term, intermediate, or long-term – but most thinking about educational aims has only been concerned with long-term objectives and has dealt, typically, with the 'kind of education' various institutions set out to provide. This use of terminology would appear to assume that a precise definition of the input to the student, normally stated in the form of the content alone, is a sufficient definition of education. Sometimes such statements have been accompanied by equally definite, not to say doctrinaire, pronouncements about the teaching methods to be used, as if educational virtue resided absolutely in specific pedagogical procedures of unchallengeable effectiveness and capable of application in any circumstances.

In Western Europe the 'input' or curricular approach to thinking about educational aims must be presumed to have its origins in the assumptions which have developed as a result of the historical development of the European universities. In the course of history an immense prestige has attached to certain subjects of study such as the ancient languages or theology. This prestige goes back to the Dark Ages when a knowledge of Latin and of the authoritative texts was not only a sign of literacy but also a passport to the priesthood and to the few prestigeful occupations then open to those of humble birth. With the slow evolution of European society over the centuries education became desirable for its own sake. The Renaissance made the study of Greek more widespread, but for the generality of students this merely broadened the basis of orthodoxy, in educational terms, and added another prestigeful subject. Ultimately, at least in England, the situation was reached where knowledge of Latin and Greek, and of something of their literatures, became the aim of education and the mark of a gentleman, for the non-theological student as well as for the priest and the scholar. Thus things at first only prestigeful because of their social and professional utility came to be of themselves totems conferring prestige; from this developed the idea that certain kinds of subject matter alone had the virtue of producing the educated man, or of training the mind to deal with the tasks presented by the not very complex administrative system for which many of the students were already destined by their social origins.

In England, the whole of higher education, except law and medicine, was concentrated in two centres, Oxford and Cambridge, until the nineteenth century. Since in the main these two universities, concerned above all with imparting instruction in the classical languages, concentrated on certain educational methods loosely called the 'tutorial method', the twin notions of classical education and of tutorial supervision came to exercise a dominant influence on thinking about higher education in England. While it is no longer true, even in Oxford or Cambridge, that the classics alone are considered essential to a complete education, the traditional ways of talking about the aims of such an education are often still used, as if nothing had changed with the passage of the centuries. The aims previously put forward as those of classical education are still to be found almost unaltered even in pronouncements about highly technical studies. In a similar way the teaching methods of the older universities are often regarded as the epitome of educational techniques, irrespective of the objectives, whether short- or long-term, which it is hoped to achieve. In this particular tradition, which at least in principle has the great virtue of taking account of the individual development of students, the stress has been on 'liberal' education, which may be defined as the general awakening and training of the intellectual faculties and the provision of a broad-based culture. Not all of this is achieved by a direct and structured educational process; the cultural elements in particular are often conveyed by a kind of environmental osmosis which unfortunately leads to certain kinds of beliefs about higher education which are not far removed from magic.

If, in this country, the Oxbridge tradition has lately been a formative influence on thinking about higher education, it has hardly been the dominant one in earlier periods of university expansion. In the middle of the last centry, when this expansion was beginning, and when the idea of a philosophy of university education took root here, there were several competing views as to the aims of such education. There were also a number of causes for the upsurge of interest in the expansion of higher education: for example, a desire for more widely spread opportunity for university education among social groups which had previously been virtually excluded from it, a demand for equal right of access to university education from religious dissenters and a call for the broadening of university studies to include the new scientific subjects. This last demand was given greater obvious urgency by the need to reaffirm the primacy of Britain as an industrial nation, and to regain the ebbing momentum of the scientific and industrial progress of countries like Germany, where the remodelled University of Berlin was leading the way in scientific research.

In England the outcome of all these various pressures, and of others besides, was the reform of the older universities, the founding of the University of London, and later of the first civic universities. The activities of the universities also underwent considerable change. The new scientific subjects, both pure and applied, became accepted, if not yet fully respectable, subjects of study, while research was recognized as a prime, and perhaps the major, duty of university teachers. This change may have been the most fundamental of all in the new university foundations of the nineteenth century, with the exception of Durham, the earliest of them. The overall result of this expansion was not to produce a number of new institutions based on the native Oxbridge model, but rather a group of new universities and colleges based more closely on continental or Scottish practice. Their chief orientation was towards the natural sciences, research was a major concern of the teachers and teaching itself was not done by the tutorial method but mainly by lectures and seminars. However, since many of the teachers and administrators in these new institutions were trained in the two ancient universities, it is not surprising that educational thinking within them, once they had acquired an impetus of their own, tended to be strongly coloured by Oxbridge ideas and attitudes. Although this was no doubt most apparent in the more traditional, non-scientific, fields of study, similar attitudes seem to have spread rapidly into scientific and even into technological disciplines.

Two main schools of thought appear to have exercised powerful and competing influences at this formative period in the development of higher education. These are usually called the 'liberal' and 'utilitarian' schools, although many mixtures of the two were, and continue to be, proposed, leading to much confusion of thought about the long-term objectives of the university. For such thinking has often been conducted on very different levels, even by the same person, so that arguments from one school are used to defend certain views of the purpose of the university, while arguments from the other may be brought in to support ideas on teaching. Although this may seem merely a typical case of British compromise, more often than not it is an attempt to reconcile inescapable social needs with traditionalism or, at worst, with nostalgic sentimentalism – an attempt to recreate a lost world of the thinker's own youth (or indeed of someone else's youth, which he himself never experienced but always envied). One result of this has been a whole world of university myths in which godlike tutors dispense gallons of sherry and coffee, and undergraduates, full of intellectual promise and eager for learning, spend sunny afternoons in punts and cosy winter evenings with the Greek philosophers or in talk such as graced the salons of eighteenth-century Paris or the Bloomsbury of Virginia Woolf. All of these and many more things of similar type form an academic Eldorado to which every boy or girl might have access (after suitably rigorous, but highly unscientific, selection) for a few golden years of youth. At the same time laurel-crowned scholars inhabit the ever-open libraries and laboratories, feast at the gourmets' high tables, and occasionally teach (by the tutorial method) a few hand-picked disciples, until such time as Minerva carries their spirits up on high (to an Olympus probably situated somewhere above the British Museum), and their earthly bodies are laid to rest beneath the flagstones of the chapel.

Satirical as this may seem, it is not very far removed from some of the writing and thinking about universities in this country since the end of the war. As wishful thinking it would be unobjectionable. What is tragic, however, is that a good deal of this mythology has found its way into many of the schemes which have actually come to reality and been supported by public money. Even worse, such a picture has often been the ideal of the university in the mind of the schoolboy or girl who comes to sit at the fount of wisdom in a grimy industrial town, where no punts ever grace the river as it meanders through concrete pipes under the railway station, or who goes to a university situated in a muddy field somewhere near a small town with two cinemas and a dance hall. In short, the need to provide more university places has been accepted, albeit grudgingly at times, but the thinking about what sort of places they should be, in terms of the kind of teaching to be offered, has been largely non-existent. It has been lost in the midst of large-scale exercises in landscape-gardening and town-planning, which too often assume that the British climate is comparable to that of California, and that students will have nothing to do but walk about in the open enjoying the visual experiences created for them. Teaching methods have usually been dealt with at the level of the catchword – this university will make the tutorial the basis of its work, that one the seminar, and so on. However, none has had the courage to say that it will use only the lecture, or do no teaching at all, although publicity material emanating from one university did seem to suggest that no teaching was to take place, since all the stress appeared to be placed on the educational value of chance encounters while walking about the campus.

In spite of all that has been said in the preceding paragraphs, a great deal of thinking has gone on about teaching methods, especially among those concerned with the new foundations. Much of this has been uninformed, however, in a very real sense, for there are no hard facts to base it upon, but only subjective impressions arising out of common experience of the frustrations of the present compared with the ideal worlds of the past. Furthermore, whether acknowledged or not, much of this thinking has had its real roots in the works of one or more of the thinkers who have written about universities in the past. These writers are not very difficult to identify; what may be difficult, however, is to disentangle the various strands of thought which emanate from each of them in the more recent pronouncements about universities (and often, by extension, about other forms of higher education). It has already been mentioned that there were two main schools of thought which influenced this thinking. To these must be added another, which is less a school of theoretical ideas than a working philosophy of the university, namely the view of the university as an intellectual powerhouse and centre for the production of knowledge.

The first of the approaches we shall consider is regarded as typically British, in certain ways, and is closely identified with the University of Oxford. This is the school of thought following from the writings of John Henry Newman; inspired by the higher education context of the mid-nineteenth century, especially in Oxford, they were largely expressed in Newman's lectures (1949), On the scope and nature of university education delivered at the Catholic University of Ireland. The second train of thought, which was certainly current at the time Newman was writing, as he testifies himself with some frequency, was the utilitarian view of higher education, whose exponents at that time wrote in the Edinburgh Review. This was, quite clearly, only an extension of that belief in social utility and material progress which had been so dominant a factor in the thought of the European Enlightenment in the late eighteenth century. The third major influence was that of the German universities of the nineteenth century, which subordinated all other functions to the extension of knowledge, (or 'research', as we now call it), an approach which paid handsome dividends in the nineteenth and early twentieth centuries, when German science and technology reached heights which surprised and startled the rest of the civilized world. None of these outlooks existed in isolation, at least in Britain.

One of the older aspects of the cult of Newman, which is often found among academics diametrically opposed to all else that the Cardinal stood for, is that his ideas on education are frequently used to defend institutions and institutional practices that are the direct opposite of what he was suggesting; but perhaps this is a true measure of the universality of his ideas. His main educational objective, or, as he himself saw it, the objective of the Roman Catholic Church in founding a university, is stated in the Preface to the lectures (1949, p. xxxvi): 'when the church founds a university, she is not cherishing talent, genius, or knowledge, for their own sake, but for the sake of her children, with a view to their spiritual welfare and their religious influence and usefulness, with the object of training them to fill their respective posts in life better, and of making them more intelligent, capable, active members of society'. As for research, Newman declares unequivocally in favour of a separate 'Academy' or research institute as the place in which knowledge is advanced. 'To discover and to teach', he says, 'are distinct functions; they are also distinct gifts, and are not commonly found in the same person'. (1949, p.xxxvii) It is not our purpose here to examine the whole of Newman's conception of the university, still less to subject it to detailed criticism. However, at this stage it may be well to remember that many of Newman's views and ideas, often indeed his very words, have passed into general discussion about universities in this country (and hardly at all in non-English speaking countries), but that they are now commonly used for purposes which may well be very far from what Newman himself meant. Certain of those ideas and phrases will be remarked upon later, and it will be seen that Newman, if he was not the real progenitor of most current ideas about the purpose of the university, at least provided much of the terminology in which these ideas tend to be expressed.

For our purposes here, however, it is necessary to stress what was for Newman undoubtedly one of the main functions of any university, whether Catholic, Protestant or secular, namely education in the liberal arts or, as he calls it, 'liberal knowledge'. This, as becomes manifestly clear in Newman's discourses, is the kind of education proposed by the reformed colleges of Oxford. It was liberal education which consciously aimed at producing the 'gentleman' (Newman does not hesitate to use the word), not through external polish, deportment and manners, but rather through the training of the intellect. This idea is the basic educational concept which informs two lectures, 'Liberal Knowledge its own end' and 'Liberal Knowledge viewed in relation to learning'. It is undoubtedly Newman who is the source of the very widespread view that a major aim of university education is to develop the individual intellect as broadly as possible with the 'liberal arts' as the core subjects of this broadening process. Basically, of course, the idea was not new, nor was it Newman's invention. It was merely the projection of the medieval system, by which the boy, who had somewhere studied Latin, went to the university and there studied the elements of knowledge, the trivium and quadrivium before going on to undertake the studies of the professional schools in theology or in the canon or civil law. Whether or not we accept Newman's views as being applicable to present-day universities and other institutions of higher learning, it is difficult to deny that most university teachers appear to act on the assumption that training the intellect, irrespective of any professional advantages which may accrue, is the real aim of an institution of higher education, as distinct from one which merely provides professional training. Once again, whether or not this is a tenable position in a mid-twentieth century context is not our real concern here. Since the purpose of this series is to discuss teaching in universities, and since many university teachers share Newman's educational objectives in a broad sense, it may be instructive to examine some of his views as to how these objectives are to be achieved.

A large part of the present series will be concerned with matters which, at first sight, do not have any apparent connection with Newman, nor even perhaps with the ways in which many teachers outside the behavioural sciences habitually view the teaching function. The concept of behavioural change often proves a difficult, if not a positively explosive one, when first introduced in discussion with groups of colleagues; indeed, in the writers' experience, it has been interjected in such discussions that the teacher is not concerned with producing 'changes in the student'. A little thought will soon make it clear that teaching is only successful when it makes the student in some way different from the person he was before, even if merely to the extent of knowing more facts, however futile these may be. If our aim is to develop the intellect to its fullest extent, then this must bring about a considerable change in the student, since by definition he will be different from one who has not had his intellect so developed. This is quite apart from any side-effects such as changes in his personality, an increase in confidence, an increase or decrease in religious or political faiths, which may have happened as a result of the basic change. At the very beginning of his book, in the Preface (1949, p. xxxviii), Newman shows that he is well aware of the role education plays in changing the student; he does not shrink from explicit recognition of this point – 'whether or no a Catholic University should put before it, as its great object, to make its students "gentlemen", still to make them something or other is its great object'. He even goes on to stress that this function of bringing about a change is the 'great object', rather than 'simply to protect the interests and advance the dominion of science'.

A little further on Newman states his objective, or rather his main educational, as distinct from propagandist, objective (although these sometimes merge), as the 'culture of the intellect', which he clearly sees as being the primary aim of liberal education. (1949, p. xl). 'Certainly', he says 'a liberal education does manifest itself in a courtesey, propriety, and polish of word and action, which is beautiful in itself, and acceptable to others; but it does much more. It brings the mind into form – for the mind is like the body'. (1949, p. xl-xli) The idea is worthy of note, if only for the fact that the very same notion is taken up again by another philosopher of university education, Ortega y Gasset, in his The mission of the university (1946), although he does not acknowledge a debt to Newman, as far as can be seen. What is important in the present context, however, is that Newman makes an analogy between body and mind which is constantly apparent as an informing principle of his attitude towards education. Many who imply that education is a mysterious process which can only be conceived in quasi-mystical terms, and in which all the factors of importance are intangible and unmeasurable, seem to be invoking Newman's ideas. Newman, himself did not exhibit this attitude. Indeed his view appears to accommodate itself well with the approaches of the behavioural sciences, even if, on occasion, he accepts conventional ideas of his time somewhat uncritically. It is also obvious, at least in his statements of overall objectives, that Newman makes a clear distinction between mental and spiritual qualities; he sees nothing untoward in adopting an attitude to the educational process which is compatible with a materialistic determination (in terms of objectives and methods), because, for him, the world of the spirit is something quite different, something that the mind can be led towards by appropriate training. It may be useful to note here that although Newman's lectures are quite openly propagandist in terms of religious intent, they are not basically concerned with ultimate questions of metaphysics or theology; these he takes for granted.

Newman makes it clear that he is concerned simply with 'the aims and principles of education' (1949, p. xliii). This is a very common approach among those who undertake to write on university education, and is certainly a far easier one than entering into more precise details of the way in which ideals are to be achieved with any certainty in teaching. Newman, however, cannot be accused of refusal to face the hard facts of the teacher-student confrontation altogether, although he declines to consider it as his true purpose in these lectures. Like most other theorists in the field, he states the subject matter which he judges appropriate to the educational objectives he has in mind and develops in some detail his reasons for including various kinds of subjects in the curriculum. What he describes is not in the least novel, nor, one assumes, are the reasons he gives very different from those any other fairly conventional educator would have given around 1850; but Newman does not baulk at the necessity for stating clearly, and in terms which might in the language of modern thought be called 'operational' or 'behavioural', just what effects he hopes liberal education will produce.

In the lecture, 'Liberal knowledge its own end', Newman speaks of knowledge and education in a way that clearly demonstrates that he does not regard them as generalized qualities which are either self-evident or defy definition, but rather as processes taking place within specified contexts and defined by enumeration of their effects. Hence : 'when I speak of knowledge, I mean something intellectual, something which grasps what is perceived through the senses; something which takes a view of things; which sees more than the senses convey; which reasons upon what it sees, and while it sees; which invests it with an idea.' (1949, p. 104) A little further on 'education' is given a meaning which once more clearly demonstrates the 'operational' nature of Newman's approach, whether or not we agree with the second part of his statement:

'Education.... implies an action upon our mental nature, and the formation of a character.' (1949, p. 105) Similarly, a little earlier, he had spoken of a university's 'treatment of its students' (our emphasis) (1949, p. 93), when talking of the habits of mind which should form in them. On the whole it would appear that such parts of Newman's thought as have passed into university theory are not those just quoted, but rather the more appealingly vague notions which are, in truth, equally plentiful in this text, such as : 'Liberal education makes not the Christian, not the Catholic, but the gentleman' (1949, p. 112), or 'Liberal education, viewed in itself, is simply the cultivation of the intellect as such, and its object is nothing more or less than intellectual excellence'. (1949, p. 113) Most academics at some time have quoted or paraphrased these words of Newman, usually with further exegesis, but very few seem to be aware that he was also conscious of the more clearly definable 'action upon our mental nature'.

Towards the end of this lecture Newman restates the aims of Liberal Education in terms which tend in the same direction as those an educational psychologist would use today, although, of course, he is rather less rigorous. He moves at least one step away from broad generalization, nearer to a set of statements of second order objectives on which an educational programme might be built, when he says : 'To open the mind, to correct it, to refine it, to enable it to know, and to digest, master, rule, and use its knowledge, to give it power over its own faculties, application, flexibility, method, critical exactness, sagacity, resource, address, eloquent expression.... ' (1949, p. 114) Each of these is an objective which could be expressed in terms of expected performance in a particular section of a discipline, and made to form the basis of a programmed course. Newman's illustration of how a tutor could bring his pupil to appreciate the manner of writing good latinity is close to the methods of the programmed approach (1929, p. 362 et seq.). Indeed it may be taken as an example of the way in which good teachers will always evolve forms of programming on their own initiative.

It is in Newman's fifth Discourse, 'Liberal knowledge viewed in relation to learning' (1949, p. 116 et seq.) that he has most to say about the detailed processes of university education. In certain ways the discourse is highly illuminating since it could be interpreted as an essay on the relationship between the quantity of knowledge communicated to the student and the quality of the intellectual training which he obtains, although the true meaning of its title appears to be the manner in which liberal education is related to the actual acquisition of both the quality and quantity of knowledge. Newman, not unexpectedly, is opposed to a mere 'cramming' with knowledge, just as he also appears to be opposed to certain forms of scholarship and erudition : 'there are authors who are as pointless as they are inexhaustible in their literary resources. They measure knowledge by bulk, as it lies in the rude block, without symmetry, without design'. (1949, p. 132) His intention is plain here : the purpose of university education is to train the intellect, not to stock it with undigested knowledge; neither is its purpose to produce scholars, as some still claim : 'Nor am I banishing, far from it, the possessors of deep and multifarious learning from my ideal university; they adorn it in the eyes of men; I do but say that they constitute no type of the results at which it aims; that it is no great gain to the intellect to have enlarged the memory at the expense of faculties which are indisputedly higher.' (1949, p. 134) Education, as Newman makes quite clear is 'the preparation for knowledge, and it is the imparting of knowledge in proportion to that preparation'. (1949, p. 137)

At this point it is evident that Newman's concept of the university owes much to his own intellectual development at Oxford; he enunciates views on university education which have come to be identified with the older British foundations and to be the ideal of very many university teachers. Essentially these are, firstly, what one may call individual attention – 'A university is, according to the usual designation, an Alma Mater, knowing her children one by one, not a foundry, or a mint, or a tread-mill' (1949, p. 137) and secondly, the view that mutual education takes place, as if by accident, through the interaction of members of a peer group. The last idea is stated by Newman in a way which makes it clear that he is reacting against certain conceptions of a university, expecially the federal examining university such as London or the Royal University of Ireland : 'I protest to you, gentlemen, that if I had to choose between a so-called university which dispensed with residence and tutorial superintendence, and gave its degrees to any person who passed an examination in a wide range of subjects, and a university which had no professors or examinations at all, but merely brought a number of young men together for three or four years, and then sent them away as the University of Oxford is said to have done sixty years since (written in 1852).... if I must determine which of the two courses was the more successful in training, moulding, enlarging the mind, which sent out men the more fitted for their secular duties, which produced better public men, men of the world, men whose names would descend to posterity, I have no hesitation in giving the preference to that university which did nothing, over that which exacted of its members an acquaintance with every science under the sun.' (1949, pp.137-138)

Unlike many who have since expressed similar ideas, Newman develops what he means by this apparent paradox of an educational institution which does no more than bring its students together. What Newman in effect does is to outline the process which had created the tradition of the older universities 'When a multitude of young persons, keen, open-hearted, sympathetic, and observant, as young persons are, come together and freely mix with each other, they are sure to learn from one another, even if there be no one to teach them; the conversation of all is a series of lectures to each, and they gain for themselves new ideas and views, fresh matter of thought and distinct principles for judging and acting, day by day.... It is seeing the world on a small field with little trouble; for the pupils or students come from very different places, and with widely different notions, and there is much to generalize, much to adjust, much to eliminate, there are inter-relations to be defined, and conventional rules to be established, in the process, by which the whole assemblage is moulded together, and gains one tone and one character.' (1949, pp. 138-139) He goes on to say that, since those who eventually occupy positions of authority in such institutions will themselves have experienced this process, which in any case is self-perpetuating, an equally self-perpetuating tradition will arise in the course of time. This Newman sees as a 'living teaching', a term which he does not define further, but which presumably means a form of teaching which is <u>living</u> because it is inherent in the environment itself. (1949, p. 139)

Whatever one may think about the universal validity of Newman's generalization from his Oxford experience, which he is here seeking to apply in the vastly different context of Catholic Ireland, it is useful to notice that he still views this in what we have called an 'operational' light; and one in which the educational experience is seen as a pattern of behavioural change resulting from the contrived environment created by bringing together young people from diverse backgrounds. Furthermore, and this may seem surprising to many in view of Newman's obvious and heavily committed position on religious and moral issues, he makes clear that he is attempting to see this matter in an objective way, looking only at the <u>educational process</u>. 'Let it be clearly understood', he says, 'I repeat it, that I am not taking into account moral or religious considerations.' (1949, p. 139) Earlier, indeed, he has gone so far as to admit that the system he is extolling had 'miserable deformities on the side of morals, with a hollow profession of Christianity and a heathen code of ethics.' (1949, p. 138), but he nevertheless discerned its educational value. At the risk of over-generalization, it may be observed that many of those who, since Newman, have sung the praises of the system he is here describing, have tended to attribute to it, explicitly or implicitly, the cultivation of these very virtues which Newman denies it. Later thinking on this matter has been, on the whole, much less rigorous. Above all, he saw processes taking place in a definite physical and intellectual environment, and tried, as far as possible in view of contemporary concepts, to define them in terms of behavioural change. However, the rigour of his thinking did not extend to a consideration of the differences in environment and culture between the society for which he was trying to legislate and that from which he drew his examples.

In several places in his '<u>Discourses</u>' Newman makes it clear that he is reacting against a certain view of education which had been inherent in the thought of John Locke in the seventeenth century, as Newman himself points out in the <u>Seventh Discourse</u>. This was put forward again with vigour in the <u>Edinburgh Review</u> during the controversy about the reform of the University of Oxford. The contrary philosophy of university education, the utilitarian view, was at that time proposed by Professor Playfair, Lord Jeffery and the Reverend Sydney Smith, three 'giants of the north' as Newman ironically calls them. He also points out that it was not an idea which had originated with them. The utilitarian view of university education needs little explanation; it consists essentially in the idea that a university should concern itself with studying and teaching those things which are useful to society as a whole. Newman quotes the writers in the <u>Review</u> as saying: 'What other measure is there of dignity in intellectual labour but usefulness?' (1949, p. 154) Adroitly, he turns this into an argument in favour of liberal education; since the aim of liberal education is the full development of the intellect of the individual; and as this enables him to play his part in society better, it follows that liberal education is <u>ipso facto</u> of the greatest utility to both the individual and society. On the whole Newman's view seems to have held sway up to the present day in all <u>discussions</u> about university education, but it is the utilitarian one which has been used as a basis for <u>action</u>, both by successive governments and by academic planners, especially those in charge of the distribution of funds.

There seems to be a strong tendency to identify a utilitarian approach to university education with a bias towards the natural sciences, although there is no reason why this need be so. Although science and technology present obvious examples of fields in which directly useful disciplines can be studied, there is no reason why many aspects of the social sciences and indeed some of the usual 'arts' subjects such as languages, should not be studied with a purely utilitarian objective in mind. The most persistent idea, however, is that of a necessary connection between natural science and utility, and this has led to the linking of the Utilitarians with those who were interested in upholding the claims of science as a subject for study. However, these thinkers, of whom Thomas Huxley (1905) was the most prominent, did not wish to see liberal studies ousted, nor to see education used merely as a means of producing people to fill specific functions. For Huxley, an education was not 'liberal' unless it contained a study of science as well as arts. In so far as the natural sciences led to a better understanding of nature, they were essential. Established authority in intellectual matters, either religious or scientific, had no hold over his mind; indeed his life was in part a quest for intellectual freedom and truth in the teeth of traditional authority. This was not a purely personal objective, but one which informed his whole thinking on education, and it probably gave him greater practical effectiveness.

Huxley considered university education a direct continuation of primary and secondary education, on both of which he had a great deal of influence. For him, every schoolboy starting at a primary school carried in his satchel a cap and gown. He was strongly opposed to a system whereby state education would produce more efficient factory operatives, while private education would send a chosen few to the university. His views were clearly informed by several factors such as egalitarianism, love of truth, opposition to imposed authority in intellectual matters, devotion to scientific method, and a conviction that the liberal arts had great value in the development of the individual. His chief educational objectives were to develop observation and reasoning; to seek the truth, and in so doing to question authority. He defined the educated man as he 'who has been so trained in youth that his body is the ready servant of his will, and does with ease and pleasure all the work that, as a mechanism, it is capable of; whose intellect is a clear, cold, logic engine, with all its parts of equal strength, and in smooth working order; ready, like a steam engine, to be turned to any kind of work, and spin the gossamers as well as forge the anchors of the mind;

whose mind is stored with a knowledge of the great and fundamental truths of Nature and of the laws of her operations; one who, no stunted ascetic, is full of life and fire, but whose passions are trained to come to heel by a vigorous will, the servant of a tender conscience; who has learned to love all beauty, whether of Nature or of Art, to hate all vileness, and to respect others as himself. Such a one, and no other, I conceive, has had a liberal education; for he is, as completely as a man can be, in harmony with nature.'

Such a view includes a great part of Newman's ideal, although it is clearly based on different personal beliefs. It adopts an essentially mechanistic view of the mind and the body, and, although it refers to spiritual and moral values, these are not based on any specific metaphysical beliefs. Here again, although perhaps to a lesser extent than in Newman's Discourses, the aims are formulated in what we have called an 'operational' manner, rather than in terms of what the liberally educated man should know, or what he should have been taught; they are expressed in terms of the result, namely what the body and the mind should be able to perform, even if these objectives are stated in very broad and general terms. These definitions differ from later ones – it would be invidious to quote examples – in that Huxley is not defining education in terms of the courses undertaken or examinations passed but rather in terms of what a 'liberally educated' man should be like at the end of it. Even so, Huxley, unlike Newman, does not give a detailed analysis of the various kinds of performance expected. The important point is that both writers are at pains to define what they mean by 'education' and do so in terms of performance; they are not content with a simple description or catalogue of mental qualities, nor do they give details of suitable curriculum, although, obviously, these would have to follow at some point if a general set of objectives were to be translated into action.

So, like Newman, Huxley was not concerned with the details of pedagogical method; however, he did have certain principles of action which must themselves have led to fairly firm conclusions about some aspects of teaching and learning. His chief concern was science, although he also gave a high place to such things as English literature, history and political economy; only science had the virtue of teaching a method of thought and action. In other words he was concerned with teaching scientific method rather than scientific facts, and for this purpose he held that teaching should come from dealing with things and not books; science teaching should follow a practical, rather than theoretical approach. An essential function of education was to make a student discover for himself as well as to think for himself. It was not enough to hypothesize and debate, a student had to be able to test his hypotheses by experiment and observation, and to reject them dispassionately if they did not fit the observations. This was the training that science gave the intellect; it had to be carried out in the laboratory and field, not in the lecture hall. Huxley was, however, concerned with wider aspects of teaching and was not content with simply stating his main objective; he held that all possible aids to teaching should be used in universities, and that their teachers should be taught both to teach and to examine.

We discover a major difference between Huxley and Newman in their views about the fundamental purpose of the university. The Catholic thinker was not convinced of the importance of research, either as a fundamental of the university or as an important function of its teachers, and saw no necessary connection between it and teaching. Huxley held opposing views. For him research was more important than teaching, the research worker was better for doing a little teaching and the teacher better for doing research; he held also that the student was better for being brought face to face with discovery and the quest for new knowledge. The difference is probably explained in terms of the different basic assumptions of the two men. Huxley was a natural scientist, keeping abreast of the great discoveries of his age, such as those of Darwin, and he clearly had a perspective of the infinitely expanding nature of science, unfettered by metaphysical restraints. Newman, on the other hand, held fast to the view that theology was the key to the ultimate truth, with which other kinds of truth must harmonize. Thus the human intellect should be trained for purposes which were ultimately metaphysical, albeit through profane knowledge, while acquisition of new truths must remain subordinate to this purpose. In spite of his conviction about the importance of research, Huxley, like Newman, did not regard the mere acquisition of knowledge as a primary aim of education. The student brought into contact with the quest for new knowledge would be fired with the idea and with the enthusiasm for truth that was more valuable than much learning.

Huxley can be identified with the Utilitarians in so far as their views coincided on the role of scientific and technical efficiency as the means of ensuring the future economic progress of the country. For this reason he tried to turn university education more firmly towards these fields of study, which no doubt also led him to adopt the view that no subject was unfit for university study, provided that it was dealt with in depth and with integrity. His definition of a university was, indeed, such that it could apply to a much broader-based institution than that thought of by Newman. 'Any corporation of men associated together for the purpose of teaching all forms of precise and accurate knowledge, the object of which was to give the highest intellectual culture that could be given, and to encourage the pursuit of knowledge in perfect freedom and without let or hindrance from any subsidiary consideration', was, said Huxley, 'performing the function of a university, and was one whatever be its name'.

Since Huxley was one of the champions of egalitarianism, he firmly held the view that everyone, regardless of religion or class background, should have a right to education at all levels, if able to profit by it. He was apparently more aware than Newman of practical requirements such as entrance qualifications; he thought that these should not be too rigid, perhaps becuase of his views on equality of access. In various other ways his ideas foreshadow the development of universities in the twentieth century rather than in his own. This shows the forward-looking approach of his thinking, even though some of the things he then foresaw are today frequently the targets of criticism. In general he may be said to have been in favour of specialization – he thought that students should not be expected to follow many courses concurrently, as this fragmented their attention, and resulted in useless cramming for examinations – 'It is important not so much to know a thing as to have known it and known it thoroughly'. 'There should not be too many subjects in the curriculum.... the aim should be the attainment of a thorough knowledge of each'. Many of his ideas, in fact, have been applied in American universities, although no direct debt to Huxley has been acknowledged. Each part of the course, he thought, should be examined before passing on to the next, instead of examining all parts at one time; this can be seen as a clear move in the direction of the 'credits' system. He also thought in terms of separate institutions concerned with General Education (Arts), Professional Education and Research, a system not unlike the Liberal Arts College, Graduate School, and Research Institutes found in many transatlantic universities. As a final point, and one on which he half agrees with Newman, Huxley wished to see a system in which the professorial (or ex cathedra) lecture system was integrated with a tutorial approach to teaching.

In terms of their ultimate objectives Huxley and Newman are probably less far apart than has sometimes been thought; where they differ considerably is in the manner of achieving these objectives and the way they assign importance to teaching and research in the overall role of the university. Huxley was not alone in thinking that science has an important part to play in education and it may be said that this view prevailed at the founding of many British 'Redbrick' universities (Huxley was present in person at the inauguration of some of them). The writings of Herbert Spencer were influential in the same direction, especially his Education: intellectual, moral and physical (1861). Spencer produces his own taxonomy of knowledge, in which he sets up specific categories – knowledge which prepares us for self-preparation, knowledge which prepares us for leisure – a clear enough set of first-order objectives. He then makes it perfectly plain that the study of natural science is to be pre-eminent: 'Whether for intellectual, moral, or religious study of grammar and lexicon'; or, in similar vein – 'What knowledge is of most worth ? – science; and as knowledge grows, and education develops, science will eventually reign supreme'. This emphasis on science, however, could be taken as a sign of the insularity of the English at that time, for universities elsewhere already believed in the pre-eminence of scientific method and in research as the primary aim of a university. This was true to some extent of the Scottish universities, but was much more the case in Germany, where several flourishing institutions, notably the University of Berlin, were already the envy of the civilized world. The influence of these universities was apparent, both in the foundation of the new English universities, and in the form that these new institutions took. Moreover, the scientific outlook was not limited to the purely scientific departments. Firmly based on the professorial system, the same outlook had spread over the whole field of knowledge, finding one of its most striking manifestations in the 'Arts' field in the work of the great German philologists, and producing an approach to such studies which Newman, although he does not expressly mention it, must have been reacting against.

It seems possible that from an amalgam of the various ideas so far discussed evolved the general objectives and philosophy on which the second generation of English universities was founded. On the whole, the example of Berlin and the ideas of Huxley and his followers prevailed, judging from the pre-eminence accorded to science, and the key position given to research. This stress on science and research, linked as it is to advancement, establishes a firm professional hierarchy in which progress is closely tied to the output of new knowledge. Consequently the teaching function is reduced to a necessary but subordinate place, very often performed in an amateur manner quite in contrast to the professional approach to research. However, Newman has remained an inspiration for academic thinkers, no doubt partly because Oxford, the source of his ideas, continued to be the most prestigeful of all universities, the one which many academics wished, and still wish to emulate. Indeed the older universities, in the main, have preserved their eminence as teaching universities, at the same time becoming highly respected research centres. However, so far they have done little to apply scientific principles to the investigation of the teaching methods they employ, preferring merely to rely on the prestige conferred by time. This prestige is not necessarily due to any proven superiority of the methods used, but rather to the fact that other institutions simply cannot afford to provide such methods on the same scale.

These, then, were the views of the great nineteenth-century thinkers on university education. Before they can be brought into perspective, the social background under which they developed must be examined. At the beginning of this era, the established church held great power in the traditional universities. Science and religion had come to a comfortable compromise, in which the former demonstrated how wondrous was the study of the latter. The two great universities of England had degenerated into what was later to be called by the Rector of Lincoln College, 'boarding schools in which the elements of the learned languages are taught to youths'. Education at this time was an adornment for those rich enough not to need to work, and therefore, the more useless their study from a practical or professional point of view, the more it emphasized how wealthy they were. Culture meant an appreciation of art, liberal education meant knowledge of the classics and intellectual development meant primarily a study of the great writers of antiquity. The concept that a man could advance knowledge by his own experiment, rather than by thought alone, had yet to develop.

Against this back cloth of a predominantly rural scene in which many laboured without formal education, while many of those who studied did not need to turn their knowledge to any account, appeared the scientist and the industrialist. The former, as exemplified by Darwin, shattered the warm coalition between church and science, and the latter became aware of the need to educate the masses in order that England could answer the challenge of the industrial age. Compulsory education and the reform of the universities followed. Both Newman and Huxley were determined that the universities should be restored to their rightful role as intellectual training grounds. However, they disagreed profoundly on the manner in which this purely intellectual development might be produced. This disagreement could be due to differences in background of the two men, although oddly enough they both went to the same school. However, whereas Newman, being an eminently successful son of a wealthy father, enjoyed a traditional public school classical education through Oxford, Huxley was forced to leave school at the age of ten because of his father's economic failure. He was subsequently self-educated. In contrast to Newman's sheltered formative years teaching at Oxford among the limited stimulus of his colleagues, Huxley worked first in the East End of London, then at medical school and finally, after qualifying, joined the navy. Newman had his traditional teachers to look up to and his classical authorities to refer to, but Huxley worked independently and defied even the Admiralty. A prolific research worker, he was Fellow of the Royal Society at twenty-five, and later its President. A practical man, his advice and help were sought at cabinet level. Newman, however, reached the lofty height of influence in other, not less influential, spheres. It is little wonder that Newman looked to heaven and to the past for inspiration, and urged his pupils to study the thoughts of the old philosophers for their intellectual betterment, whereas Huxley urged them to stand on their own feet and look forward to the next century of discovery, and to sharpen their wits on scientific method. Inevitably, the tradition of Newman passed over into an era where tradition is still valued for its own sake, but it was also inevitable that this would be tempered by the clear sight of a man like Huxley. By reason of his great power and deeds he could speak with equal authority at Oxford, Baltimore or a working man's club and so left his mark on the minds of his fellow-countrymen.

Following the heyday of Newman and Huxley, thinking about university education was not very active for several decades after the turn of the century. However, just before and just after the Second World War two new treatises on university education were produced, the first in Spain by Ortega y Gasset, and the other in Germany by Karl Jaspers. Both these works, more than any other of the present century, have been quoted in recent debates on the philosophy of university education although neither of them does much more than restate fundamental positions originating from Newman and Huxley, or derived from existing continental practice. However, very clearly stated in Ortega's <u>The mission of the university</u> (1946) is a point of view precisely opposite to that of Huxley and most members of the academic profession about research and teaching going hand in hand and teachers having to take part in research : 'Knowledge and research have their own structure, which is not applicable to that other activity proposing to impart knowledge. The principle of pedagogy is entirely different from that on which culture and science are built.' Not only is Ortega prepared to state this unequivocally, but he also provides a rationale for university teaching, or presumably any other kind, based on the view that education has 'with peculiar blindness, centred about knowledge and the teacher', rather than about the learner. He cites Rousseau, Pestalozzi, Froebel and the German Idealists to support his view that all education should be centred on the characteristics of the learner; this he says, 'alone can guide us in our effort to make something organic of education.

In a manner reminiscent of Herbert Spencer he holds that 'man is occupied and preoccupied with education and for a reason which is simple, bald, and devoid of glamour : in order to live with assurance and freedom and efficiency, it is necessary to know an enormous number of things'; to this he adds his characteristic argument, 'and the child or youth has an extremely limited capacity for learning.' This favourite, though frequently overlooked, point is reinforced later : 'Scarcity of the capacity to learn is the cardinal principle of education. It is necessary to provide for teaching precisely in proportion as the learner is unable to learn.' Moreover, says Ortega, knowledge is growing so fast that we must operate on the principle of economy in education; our science of teaching must be based on the simple idea that the student cannot learn all that we should like him to know. This puts the onus on the teacher to select material and to match it with his knowledge of the learning capacity of the student. Although this rule has always been in operation, he says, wherever there has been teaching activity, it had never been set up as a principle 'perhaps because at first sight it is not dramatic – it does not talk of imposing transcendentals.' Developing his argument Ortega continues 'The university of today, outside Spain even more than within, is a tropical underbrush of subject matters.... There is no remedy but to rise up against this turgid undergrowth and use the principle of economy like a hatchet. First of all a thorough pruning.' He then proceeds to extend his principle from the teaching situation to the organization of the university itself, which must 'be based upon the student, and not upon the professor or upon knowledge'; it must be the projection of the student to the scale of the institution. And the student's two 'dimensions' are, first, what he is – a being of limited learning capacity – and second, what he needs to know in order to live his life. The principle of the student university is not new, as Ortega himself is quick to point out -

it is a return to the type of organization existing originally at Bologna in the Middle Ages – but he gives it a new twist by linking it with his pedagogical principle that teaching must be geared to learning capacity. This principle is certainly found in many modern paradigms of the learning situation, as well as in Rousseau, and other earlier thinkers who based their arguments on common sense rather than experimental evidence.

The other writer of whom we have spoken is Karl Jaspers (1960). To him the university is 'an institution uniting those professionally dedicated to the quest and transmission of truth in scientific terms.' Later he states unequivocally that 'research is the foremost concern of the university.... the university's second concern is teaching; because truth must also be transmitted.' Jasper's approach to the whole subject of teaching is made up for the most part of a series of seemingly authoritative statements relying on no other evidence than traditional use. He is not concerned with the majority of students : 'University education addresses itself not to the few geniuses or to the mediocre average, but to that minority who while capable of growth and of initiative, nevertheless stand in need of instruction.'

Some of the present day talk and discussion about university teaching tends to sound rather as if it were based on the writings of Karl Jaspers, so full is it of crude assertions about method and untested assumptions about students (in the Anglo-Saxon context these assumptions seem much less flattering to the students than do the more idealistic ones frequently made by Jaspers). Nevertheless there is still much current ideology which has its roots in Newman and Huxley. While Huxley and Jaspers share the research based conception of the university – they almost certainly derived it from the common source of nineteenth-century Germany - Huxley has probably played a large part in forming the purely scientific frame of mind which is hostile to professional training in British universities. Newman also contributed to this attitude, but he added the idea of the 'gentleman', an idea always lurking somewhere in the British academic mind. Also he undoubtedly helped to strengthen the idealized view that Oxford practices in teaching should be the ultimate aim. It is to Newman and Ortega y Gasset that people have turned since the war, to find views and ideas for the debate on liberal education. This has resulted in many different theories and even in actual educational schemes, so that these thinkers have had considerable influence on the academic planning of certain of the newer universities. It is surprising, and also rather regrettable, that they have been raided for their general ideas, their views on the ethos of a university and of its objectives in the broadest sense, but not for their way of stating more limited objectives, those of the teaching process itself. Newman, Huxley and Ortega y Gasset seem to have discovered the keystone on which the whole edifice must be built – the fact that education must, by definition, be seeking to produce a behavioural change in the learner. Ortega y Gasset goes even further in that he seeks to build his whole university around the learner and his limitations. Although none of them was an expert, in the modern sense, on pedagogical method, they all saw the need to define their objectives in a manner which is not too far removed from that of an educational psychologist of today.

Chapter 3 A PSYCHOLOGIST'S APPROACH TO DEFINING OBJECTIVES

Ruth M. Beard

1 INTRODUCTION

Unlike the philosophers whose views have been discussed in Chapter 2, psychologists are concerned primarily with methods of planning activities to promote learning. Their aim is to assist teachers in selecting from the many possible objectives in such a way that time and resources can be used effectively and economically. They attempt to develop a programme for teaching, learning and evaluation which will ensure achievement of the chosen objectives. Even before they have attempted to make these explicit, teachers are normally aware of certain general aims of their courses; they have fairly clear cut views as to what constitutes a satisfactory degree of mastery of the subject matter and, if it seems relevant, may already take into account future professional requirements. It is not usually the function of the psychologist to assist the teacher in determining his general, long-term aims – for instance the professional skills required by a doctor or statistician; but once these have been decided by experts in the field on professional, social and philosophical grounds, the psychologist may help to organize and to phrase them more clearly, to provide intermediate goals in order to maintain students' interest, to design learning programmes and to devise methods to determine whether the objectives are realized.

Inadequate definition of intermediate objectives has fairly easily recognized consequences : among students it results in loss of motivation which reveals itself by lack of interest, putting off tasks to the last moment, questioning the value of the course as a whole, or even by forthright criticism; whereas in the case of their teachers it is seen in frustration to the unco-operative attitude of students and in the belief that students desire the rewards which a degree will bring them without undertaking the work. As an instance, a teacher of clinical medicine mentioned to his students in the introductory course that they should observe 'patient care' and that it would be examined in finals – three years later; he was surprised to find that they made little attempt to observe it until shortly before the final examination. A psychologist would certainly suggest some intermediate objectives here. To mention only a few possibilities : he might use a questionnaire directing students to particular kinds of observations by means of carefully framed questions with space for additional observations; or students could be asked to record their observations during a period of a few weeks prior to a general discussion or, again, individuals in the group might be asked to observe particular aspects of patient care with the object of reporting them to the whole group. For several reasons, the first of these alternatives would be likely to prove most efficient in the long run : firstly, the teacher could ensure that everything important was covered; secondly, an active response increases interest and makes memorizing easier; and thirdly, if correct answers were made available, each student would have an accurate record for revision.

Statements of aims without relating them to teaching methods or arranging for their evaluation is almost equally inadequate. Miller (1962) reported of the Medical Schools in Illinois in the 40's that an aim high on the list in the prospectus was development of critical thinking, but teachers observed in seminars talked for more than 75 per cent of the time and questions were not encouraged. When results in tests of critical thinking were compared with grades given in the medical department it appeared that the 25 students who thought most critically had more faulty grades than the least critical 25. Similarly, in a study in the United States of a large number of colleges, Jacob (1957) found that although teachers believed that they influenced students' attitudes there was no evidence of change in students' values, beliefs or personalities. But in an experiment where new methods of teaching were set up to inculcate an interest in comprehensive medical care the experimental group showed a superior attitude in this respect to the control group (Hammond and Kern 1959).

Unlike knowledge and skills, which once mastered are not easily forgotten, changes in attitudes may prove relatively impermanent. A recent study by McFarlane Smith (1973) of mature student teachers of technical subjects at Garnett College showed that their attitudes changed very considerably in the desired direction (from authoritarian to democratic) during the year of training; but the majority of them reverted to their earlier views after serving for one year as teachers in schools and colleges. A variety of hypotheses can be suggested as to why this should be so. Many teachers in colleges and Departments of Education would argue that it happened because conditions in the schools are so far from ideal that new teachers find it almost essential to accept the authoritarian views of their older colleagues in order to survive. Conceivably, however, it is only what the students say about teaching methods which is influenced in their course; the ways in which they deal with children may not be fundamentally altered; if this is so, their views are likely to change again in line with their behaviour. Or perhaps the attitudes are unrealistic and children prefer strict teachers? Or possibly, the students whose attitudes are most influenced in college are the more suggestible individuals who can therefore be expected to be influenced, in turn, by their new colleagues. Thus a finding such as this should stimulate further inquiry, above all with a view to influencing attitudes more permanently. In addition, the results of further investigation may influence the objectives of teachers in the college and the ways in which they frame them.

Where no clear-cut aims are previously agreed, inquiry suggests that in any one department the aims and teaching methods of the staff may differ widely. Studies by Walton and Drewery (1964) showed the existence of no less than four types of aim among 21 teachers of psychiatry. Although all the teachers aimed to provide systematic information, this was the exclusive goal of three of them; six others, in addition, taught with a psycho-dynamic orientation; seven shared these goals but also aimed to teach behavioural science; while the remaining five included as a fourth aim to modify the behaviour of students. On examination of their specialities it proved that hospital staff lecturers tended to have aims of the first two kinds while academic lecturers favoured the last two, the difference between them in this respect being significant. A further significant difference was found between lecturers with a combined subject orientation (usually academic lecturers) who had scientific and behaviour modifying goals, whereas those with a unidimensional subject orientation had information goals only. Thus although there may be latitude for variety in aim and method among staff members in teaching different topics, and it is conceivable that their varied approaches may be beneficial to students by providing for different interests, it is nevertheless essential to know what biases exist if a well directed teaching programme is to be devised.

In addition to differences between staff, those between students must also be considered if objectives are to be defined which will make teaching fully effective. The students' levels of development on entry to a course must be taken into account together with their different abilities and approaches to study. The investigation of Jahoda and Thomas (1966) shows that students differ in their aims in learning and that they employ a variety of techniques in studying which may be more or less effective. The suggestion of the authors, that staff should spend time early in the course on individual tutoring, encouraging students to examine their learning processes in order to save time later and to increase the students' range of learning, points to a new way of achieving effective learning which has hardly been looked at even in schools where teachers are much concerned to make their courses effective.

A further factor which must be taken into account in outlining objectives is the changing situation with regard both to subject matter and to the introduction of new techniques of teaching. The rapidity with which most scientific subjects develop and change suggests the importance of stressing principles and how to apply them, rather than concentrating on acquisition of information. New techniques allow greater efficiency in various aspects of teaching – large numbers may be simultaneously taught by television, or individuals can repeat work privately using tapes, or tapes combined with visual aids. Demonstrations formerly visible to a few individuals can now be shown to hundreds while a difficult topic which used to require the aid of a teacher may be programmed into sufficiently small stages for the least able student to tackle it alone. Investigations by psychologists show the advantages of all these techniques in various circumstances. Since both developments in subject matter and in teaching techniques are likely to continue with increasing momentum, frequent review of aims in teaching will almost certainly become necessary.

As soon as goals such as memorizing of information, grasp of principles, mastery of skills, acquisition of a scientific attitude, independence, and so on, have been decided on, numerous questions are raised with regard to teaching methods and evaluation. Are different teaching methods required to achieve different aims? For example, can critical thinking be encouraged as readily in lectures as in group discussions? How does a student learn to work independently – by reading, use of programmed books, preparation of a dissertation, by solving problems or by some other means? And, where the aim is acquisition of information, how can it be achieved most efficiently, ensuring maximum retention of the facts in the minimum time? Further, by what means should the success of teaching methods be evaluated? And how are we to maintain the students' interest or even to increase their output of productive work?

2 THE SCHOOLS OF PSYCHOLOGY

It is important to realize that the main families of psychologists differ essentially in the educational aims they set up as well as in the means they use to achieve them. The schools derive from two different experimental approaches to the study of problem solving - that of the Gestalt School and of Thorndike's 'Connectionism'. In the 1920's the Gestalt psychologists experimented with apes, allowing them experience of playing with sticks or boxes, prior to setting them problems by putting a 'reward' such as a banana out of reach. Apes who had had appropriate play experiences were at first puzzled but then suddenly realized the possibilities of using their toys to reach the inaccessible fruit, even fitting sticks together or piling boxes into towers. Thorndike, on the other hand, experimented by putting cats in boxes which could be opened by pressing a lever. The random movements of the cat eventually led to its chance escape, but on successive occasions, the escape occurred increasingly early although the cat could not be said to have learned to control the escape mechanism. It was this difference in approach which led Bertrand Russell to comment 'Animals studied by Americans rush about frantically, with an incredible display of hustle and pep, and at last achieve the desired result by chance. Animals observed by Germans sit and think, and evolve the solution from their inner consciousness'.

Today field psychologists think of behaviour as a function of the total situation. It is impossible to say to what extent behaviour is influenced by physiological or environmental factors; but both of these, including health and personality as well as the influence of other persons and the individual's view of himself, must be taken into account in trying to modify his goals or motivate him to learn. They describe learning in terms of the individual sizing up, or interpreting, his world in a way that is meaningful to him, integrating experiences into existing organizations of knowledge, and using his environment in ways advantageous to him. It follows that what the individual perceives is selective. In teaching, therefore, they are concerned with motivation, stress the importance of arranging that learning experiences are organized into meaningful wholes, and favour the use of problem situations which enable to learner to gain 'insight' as he suddenly realizes how to use information or how to interpret it meaningfully. In addition, the learner may develop and follow his own goals. The associationists, on the other hand, reject any introspective concepts such as 'goal' or 'insight' and concentrate their attention on changes in behaviour. They describe learning as built up by reinforcement of responses to stimuli in the environment. Consequently, it was not at first thought necessary that the learner should wish to learn but only that the teacher should encourage him to follow a logically organized sequence of stimuli, feedback as to his success serving to reinforce correct responses. But the recent distinction between 'effective stimuli' for those relevant to the needs of the learner and 'non-effective stimuli' for those which are not is a modification which may open the way to allow for individual differences such as interests and motivations. Broadly, therefore, field psychologists concentrate attention on the learner, his attitudes, goals and interests, whereas associationists are more concerned with the structure of the subject matter.

Major contributions to the study of objectives have been made by psychologists of the associationist school in defining aims for the purposes of preparing objective tests or in planning programmes for teaching machines or programmed books. In both cases the psychologist begins by stating what behaviour the learner should be capable of at the end of a course or learning programme. For example, the vague aim 'to understand hypoglycaemia' is replaced by more specific statements such as: 'to list four principal causes of hypoglycaemia, to recognize the difference between acute and chronic cases, to describe the changes in the brain, to understand the mechanism, to list the minor causes, to differentiate between the lesions of acute and chronic hypoglycaemia' (Moore 1954). Since the expert in the field tends to take these points for granted when he sees them (though he is usually rather slower to produce them), and it is only the student or someone less familiar with the field who immediately sees the advantage of having objectives spelled out in this way, we will give a similar break-down in other subjects. Croxton and Martin (1965) who have prepared some forty programmes in strength of materials and theory of structures used the following objectives in a three and a half hour programme on 'axially loaded structural members made from two materials having different elastic and thermal properties':

1 To recognize that the problem cannot be solved by statistics alone and to understand the meaning of the term 'statistically indeterminate'.

2 For a particular example with external axial loading:

   a to sketch a free body diagram;

b to form an equation from statics;

c to form an equation from the 'geometric fit' and to understand the meaning of the term 'compatibility';

d to form an equation from Hooke's Law;

e to solve these equations to find the stresses in the two materials.

3 To solve similar problems extending the method to the consideration of thermal effects and 'lack of fit'.

4 To solve more general problems using the same principles but which have more complex or unfamiliar configuration.

If, in this case, clear statement of objectives is no aid because the subject is so unfamiliar as to be meaningless, objectives in a section of elementary statistics should convince the reader that it is helpful to have exact requirements stated. J. Newsom of Nottingham suggests the following aims in studying reliability and validity. We must assume that his students are already acquainted with 'correlation'.

1 To distinguish between <u>validity</u> and <u>reliability</u> by defining each but noting that each can be expressed as a coefficient of correlation.

2 To distinguish different types of <u>validity</u>:

a face validity;

b predictive validity;

c criterion validity (including method of criterion groups);

d construct validity (including factorial validity).

3 To distinguish different types of <u>reliability</u>:

a test-retest (consistency);

b parallel forms;

c split halves (including Kuder Richardson).

4 To note the relative advantages and disadvantages of these alternative methods and conditions under which each would be appropriate.

5 To discuss the relationship between reliability and validity, and the way each is affected by 'test length', homogeneity of standardization sample, speed vs. difficulty, etc.

Newsom remarks that 'even with these aims it would be possible to cover the subject at different levels according to the statistical sophistication of the students'.

Although this way of defining aims was first devised by the associationists, it does not preclude a student-centred approach in teaching; for, if the student himself is acquainted with so clear a list of objectives for every topic in the syllabus, together with a list of references and has access to visual aids and specimens, it is possible for him to teach himself. Indeed, where this has been arranged, with free discussions between students, or between students and staff, as well as time set aside for periods of group discussion, students have acquired more information about a topic with more interest and in appreciably less time than by conventional methods (Erskine and Tomkin 1963). But the same objectives could serve equally in devising a carefully sequenced programmed book which all students would follow in the same order, if it was linear; or, again, they might be used to guide a more conventionally planned programme of lectures, demonstrations and individual study.

From these considerations it is evident that objectives in teaching are to some extent a matter of choice; teachers may choose to follow the field psychologists by maximizing interest and teaching through problem situations, or the associationists in providing a carefully sequenced programme of learning, or they may follow the practice of many teachers and use either method with different aims in mind on different occasions. But, whichever they do it will be advantageous to describe fairly exactly in what ways the teaching procedure should alter the behaviour of the students.

Teachers who wish to specify their objectives more clearly can obtain help from the categories and illustrative examples in the Taxonomy of educational objectives by Bloom and his associates (1954, 1956); from categories similar to these such as those of McGuire (1963) and Scriven (1967); from books written to guide teachers or instructors in preparing learning programmes, eg. Bloom, Hastings and Madeus (1971), Davies (1971), Kibler, Barker and Miles (1970), or outlines of objectives for particular courses in higher education, eg. in medicine,

Naeraa's Objectives for a course in physiology for medical students (1972) A list of medical objectives, including a 500 page book of objectives for the clinical course at Illinois, is available from the Director of the British Medical Association Department of Audio-Visual Communication.

3 ANALYSES OF OBJECTIVES

Bloom and his associates (1954, 1956) made detailed analyses of categories of objectives in the cognitive and affective fields with a view to their use as goals in instruction and, in the case of cognitive goals, to ensure the adequate representation of different aspects of knowledge and understanding in objective tests. Formation of a hierarchy of objectives in the cognitive domain proved fairly straightforward, for the defining abilities had received considerable attention from evaluators who had already identified the kinds of behaviours to be tested. In this domain, therefore, educational behaviours are arranged in order from simple to complex, in the belief that in the course of an individual's mental development a particular simple behaviour may become integrated with other simple behaviours to form a more complex behaviour. For consistency, each behaviour is placed in the most complex class which is appropriate and relevant. This provides a single order whether the reader accepts the view of the field psychologists, in particular those of the Gestalt School, that complex behaviour is something more than the sum of simpler behaviours, or the associationist view that the sum follows the usual laws of addition. However, it cannot overcome the difficulty in testing an individual that the nature of his prior educational experience influences the complexity of the test to him; thus a test item which is a matter of simple recall to a student who has previously studied this type of problem requires a complex solving ability on the part of someone wholly untrained. This of course partly undermines the value of the classificatory system.

Other criticisms have been raised by two philosophers. Sockett (1971) points out that this taxonomy fails to distinguish between general and specific objectives; there is no place in it for a general objective such as 'getting children to understand society'. Although he is not against detailed analyses of what children arc to learn, he feels that this is a taxonomy of educational processes rather than of objectives. Pring (1971) is concerned about the division it makes between cognitive and affective objectives for, he says : 'to think scientifically entails a concern – a feeling if you like – for the standards of scientific truth'. He also dislikes the distinction made between knowledge and understanding what it means to say that something is the case. 'To know that something is the case entails understanding what it means to say that something is the case and this, in turn, entails being able to apply this knowledge to particular situations.' Thus, he considers that through lack of any epistomological analysis of cognitive processes, the taxonomy makes false distinctions.

The cognitive continuum, as described by Bloom and his associates, begins with the students' recall and recognition of knowledge such as terminology, dates and events, conventions, symbols, methods, structures and so on. Although this is influenced by previous knowledge and by a conceptual framework – as we see if we attempt to learn symbols in our familiar alphabet or in a wholly foreign one such as Chinese – nevertheless, in testing, this objective normally requires little more than recall of information. Where higher cognitive objectives are not specified in teaching and testing there is a tendency to concentrate effort on this category and simpler kinds of comprehension. Since memorizing information involves somewhat different approaches in teaching from the acquisition of mental abilities and skills, it is of importance to clearly distinguish them. The latter differ in that the learner has acquired a capacity to do something with his knowledge other than merely to recall it. He learns to reorganize information or a problem, for example, or to use information in dealing with new problems and situations. All subsequent objectives may therefore be described as cognitive skills or abilities.

This category is often criticized by those who attempt to employ it. After using a similar category of McGuire's (1964), based on that of the Bloom Taxonomy, Beard and Pole (1971) comment 'McGuire's first category, "recall of specific facts", for example, seems to imply a range of activities from "isolated recall" to "knowledge of concepts and principles", but there is no provision for knowing about the numerous relationships between those concepts and principles, from which is built a structured body of knowledge. Indeed, there is no attempt to distinguish between a body of knowledge capable of growth and an agglomeration of parts which may reasonably be expected to deteriorate. A well ordered body of knowledge raises expectations about the material world, and so also gives rise to questions about causality, explanations about phenomena or alternative explanations. It is therefore not a close system but one which offers possibilities for development. When a student is asked to reproduce it, he can call on a pattern, or structure, and does not merely list items of information. This distinction has not been made by those who specified categories and, since it has not been spelled out, there is a danger that it will not be recognized in teaching. Students often complain that they are simply offered masses of detailed information which they memorize and regurgitate in examinations, but which they promptly forget.'

The second objective of Bloom and his associates is that of comprehension. A student shows comprehension if he can translate from one medium to another, eg. from a map to a model, from a formula to the statement of a principle, from symbols or diagrams to a verbal description, etc. Or he may go beyond the data he was given, by interpolating missing data in a graph, making inferences from a passage he has read or generalizing from specific instances. Or again, he can extrapolate by predicting further events in a sequence or by suggesting consequences of actions.

The third category of objectives is concerned with application of information. This differs in kind from comprehension because it involves appreciation of the nature of a problem and, possibly, restructuring it to solve it by know procedures. It is a common difficulty among poorer students of mathematics, for example, that although they comprehend relevant principles they are unable to apply them to any but familiar types of problem. However, if problems are complex and unfamiliar their solution involves abilities from a higher category of objectives.

The fourth and fifth categories, though different in kind are needed together for the solution of unfamiliar and difficult problems. In the first place, the student must analyse the problem into its constituent parts, recognizing relationships between them. The ability to analyse is needed whether the problem arises in mathematics, chemistry, relations within a group of people or from a study of a patient's symptoms prior to making a diagnosis. In the second place the problem solver is usually required to synthesize his findings, together with information from other sources, to form a meaningful whole, or solution, to his problem. However, each of these skills could be employed separately : in a chemical problem analysis may be all that is required whereas in writing an essay for which the information is already available from different sources the main problem is one of synthesis.

Finally, the sixth cognitive objective, evaluation, involves the making of judgments for some purpose concerning the value of information, ideas, methods of treatments and materials, etc. The evaluation may be concerned with external criteria of efficiency, economy or utility of specific means to attain a particular end, or it may be relative to internal standards of excellence such as consistency and accuracy of logical rigour.

Contrasted with acquisition of knowledge, the cognitive skills and abilities more readily transfer to other situations. Consequently, teaching which introduces information as something to be learned with minimal thought is inefficient compared with that which, from the beginning, emphasizes relationships, understanding of principles and their application, or their use in solution of problems. In addition, rapid advances in the scientific field put a premium on cognitive abilities and skills rather than information, because it is they which transfer to the understanding and use of new information or of new branches of knowledge. Further, there is increasing need for creative workers in science and technology who can go beyond the solution of familiar kinds of problems to the development of original syntheses. Although such an attitude is probably inborn or developed early in life, there is no doubt that teaching could foster it by provision of 'open-ended' problems and opportunities for students to work at problems of their own choosing. Moreover, their choice of problems and the method of dealing with them should enable teachers to recognize in a greater number of students some capacity for original work. It is of interest that expectation on the part of an employer or teacher that scientists or students will produce original work in itself results in their doing so, provided, of course, that the expectation is expressed. Gordon (1961), in his book on Synectics, mentions a firm in which a team of scientists failed to produce sufficient inventions for patent to justify their existence or to keep the firm flourishing. They concerned themselves with pure science and were not very productive. When it was suggested to the manager that he should tell them what he required, and he did so, a rapid stream of inventions followed. Similarly, with students, just giving them opportunity for originality and showing that it is valued appears to result in an increased output of original work (Hayes 1964). It is well known that some degree examinations can be passed very creditably by individuals with exceptionally retentive memories but little creative talent, whereas some of those capable of outstanding originality fail to do well. Poorer graduates could be selected as research workers if it was already known that they could go beyond familiar and partial solutions and stay with a problem, trying varied procedures on it, until they arrived at genuine and original solutions.

The affective domain necessarily impinges on the cognitive one. A student may find it impossible to analyse a problem objectively if it touches on his personal prejudices or if he has developed an emotional block towards it perhaps from discouragement; and he is unlikely to become a creative worker if his personality is such that he adheres inflexibly to views, standards or approaches which he has accepted from his teachers. Affective states are, of course, continuously operative among all students when learning, no matter how ostensibly intellectual the content of their studies. Inescapable evidence of failure to solve mathematical problems for instance, is one of the most traumatic experiences to students who suffer it frequently. Demonstrable failure tends to depress effort, whereas success, or promise of success, and methods of teaching which give rise to a series of partial problems with sufficient hints to help the learner to recall or discover the principles which solve them, lead to increased application and interest. Training students to work independently, to solve their own problems, to extend or reorganize their knowledge as new developments are made, and so on, therefore inevitably involves affective objectives.

It is of interest that Bloom and his associates had difficulty in defining objectives in the affective domain partly because comparatively little evaluation had been undertaken within it (Bloom 1956). It would seem that although their equation 'objectives = behaviours = evaluation techniques = test problems' was arrived at by equating certain behaviours, the equation is genuinely reciprocal; that is to say, if evaluative procedures cannot be found, the behaviours are wrongly described and the objective is spurious or so general as to be meaningless. Nevertheless, to test affective behaviours reliably presents greater difficulties than the evaluation of cognitive behaviours.

The most important affective objective is the increase of motivation, or the inner incentive to learn. Various methods of doing this are in use: writers of programmed books provide many short term aims and reinforcement via immediate correction of the students' responses, whereas followers of the field psychologists set up problems for students to solve or involve them in projects which are of interest to them. But, in either case, motivation in learning is influenced by realization that the work set will serve the students' ultimate goals and it will be increased by successful realization of intermediate goals.

The hierarchy of affective objectives as outlined by Bloom and his associates is determined by the degree of internalization of the affective state, ranging from a merely passive receptivity to organization of values into a coherent whole characterizing the individual. As a value becomes increasingly accepted by an individual, he attends more actively to it, perhaps showing appreciation by an observation or comment. A second objective is that he should respond actively although initially the stimulus is an external one – he visits the museum, reads the assigned literature, or completes his homework; but as he grows more involved, he increases his activities voluntarily and obtains satisfaction from doing so. The third objective is that the learner should come to accept a value such as developing a continuing determination to speak and write effectively, an appetite for what is good in literature or the wish to achieve accurate and well developed argument in writing a report. The fourth objective is that the student should organize his values into some kind of internally consistent system until, finally, the fifth objective is attainable – that of integration of his beliefs, ideas and attitudes into a total philosophy or world view. At this level there is inevitably a cognitive component; for the individual is accepting a value – that something is good for him and this is a judgment which goes beyond affect.

Probably the majority of teachers would feel that they should attempt to aid the student in the achievement of these objectives up to the third, but, unless teaching philosophy, might feel that the fourth and fifth objectives were outside the province of the university teacher. It is generally hoped that the university will provide the environment in which mature attitudes can be achieved and that the students will develop them, while attempts on the part of teachers to indicate a desirable integration of beliefs and values into a total philosophy would normally be regarded as propaganda. As we have seen, this involves consideration of the nature of education and the role of the teacher.

The findings of Inhelder and Piaget (1959) concerning the thinking of adolescents suggest that the establishment of what he terms 'formal operations' at the age of about 16 years involves a hypothetico-deductive method of thinking and the reference of opinions and judgments to general principles of behaviour. However, university teachers must be aware that these mature modes of thinking are by no means fully established in many students, so that the question remains whether it should be an objective at this level to induce students to think and feel in a mature fashion on a wide range of problems. The studies of Walton and Drewery (1964, 1966) show that the views of teachers are likely to differ, but we cannot set aside the problem of immature thinking in students destined for professions in which they influence other members of the public or are called on to make responsible decisions.

4 DEFINING SPECIFIC BEHAVIOURAL OBJECTIVES

The discussion about objectives so far has been limited almost exclusively to general ones which, as we saw in Chapter 1, are used in outlining courses and curricula. Specification of objectives, in much more detail and in terms of behavioural changes which supply standards for evaluation, is an essential stage in planning programmed texts, and similar well organized programmes, employing audio-visual aids. But as Furst (1957) points out in discussing the analysis of general objectives 'To communicate the right meaning to other interested persons, such as students or colleagues, the analysis should be carried to the point where they will know what specific behaviours to accept as evidence of the larger attribute'. Thus, for the sake of clarity, behavioural objectives should be specified wherever it is possible. It is a common practice for educational technologists when writing articles and books to communicate to their readers the objectives which they hope will be achieved. For instance Davies in his book The management of learning, (1971), specifies his objectives at the beginning of each chapter and provides a brief post-test at its conclusion to enable the reader to check his learning. At the beginning of Chapter 5 on Writing Objectives, he provides the following learning objectives :

Cognitive objectives

After carefully reading this chapter, you will be able to :

1 distinguish between an aim and an objective;

2 state four reasons for specifying objectives;

3 recognize, and discriminate between, cognitive, affective and psychomotor objectives;

4 list four ways in which Bloom's taxonomy can be useful to the teacher or instructor;

5 state what words should be avoided and what words should be used when writing clear objectives;

6 list, and write short notes upon, the three types of information essential to a clear objective;

7 write a clear objective using either the Mager or the Miller system.

Affective objectives

After reading this chapter, the author intends that you will :

1 be aware of, and value, the importance of clear objectives to the learning process;

2 incorporate into your teaching behaviour either the Miller or the Mager system of writing objectives. '

These objectives serve to alert the reader to the most important points and to increase the probability that he will attempt to recall them or to consider in what ways he could apply them. Addition of a post-test virtually ensures mastery of the subject matter, at least in the short term.

Specific, or behavioural objectives, are usually framed in accordance with Mager's recommendations (1962), ie. they describe the behaviour which the learner would be required to employ in demonstrating mastery of the objectives (eg. to write, to state, to select,); list important conditions under which the reader should be able to demonstrate his achievement (eg. time limit, with what material or equipment); and state criteria which would be used to evaluate his performance (eg. to distinguish between, to state several criteria, or the percentage success in a test if this seems relevant).

Similarly, in planning an activity for student teachers, Kibler, Barker and Miles (1970) give criteria for satisfactory performance :

'Micro Teaching - teach a concept

The pre-service teacher will teach a single concept and evaluate whether or not it has been learned within a period of seven minutes.

A critique of the presentation will be made by the class members in terms of the learning activities selected to bring the referent to the students, amount of student involvement, whether or not the concept was learned and the voice, poise and mannerisms of the teacher. He will summarize the suggestions made for improvement and state those he would select for implementation and the steps he would take to implement them.

Micro-teaching: reinforcing student behaviour

While teaching a seven minute concept lesson, the pre-service teacher will demonstrate positive ways to reinforce desirable student behaviour. The demonstration will include at least four different appropriate ways of providing positive reinforcement and must involve directly a majority of the members of the micro-class.'

If a skill or ability can be described in these exact and comprehensive ways, the methods advocated by educational technologists ensure that its different aspects are rehearsed, whilst the learner, and perhaps his teacher, know to what extent he is succeeding. It seems to be mainly in the sciences that these methods are sometimes appropriate. In London University, for example, chemists are co-operating in writing and testing programmed texts (Beard 1972); and at the BMA Department of Audio-Visual Communication, Engel and his colleagues are preparing and collecting carefully planned books to be used with tapes and tests which enable young doctors to teach themselves, for instance, how to treat cardiac failure in the hospital ward (Zorab et al. 1972). Some behavioural objectives for this course are as follows:

'A Clinical competence – Cardiac Arrest Under hospital ward conditions, the resident house officer will be able to demonstrate that he can

1 diagnose cardiac arrests;

2 initiate and carry out cardiac massage and artifical ventilation;

3 initiate and assist at

i improving ventilation;

ii ECG interpretation;

iii drug therapy;

iv defibrillation;

4 decide when resuscitation measures ought not to have been instituted;

5 assess when cardiac massage can cease'

Examples of behavioural objectives in the natural sciences and humanities are given in Evaluation in higher education by Paul Dressel and associates (1961). A book by Dressel and Mayhew (1956) will also be of interest to teachers of humanities.

Teachers wishing to plan courses in this way may be tempted to begin by defining objectives at the behavioural level since they also provide criteria for evaluation. However, Scriven (1967) warns against this on the grounds that there is a tendency to limit the course to content for which such objectives are most easily defined. He recommends beginning by defining objectives at a 'conceptual level' which conveys to the student what his views of the subject should be, and employs a 'manifestational level' which specifies the kind of skills or improvements in learning which result from study. The 'operational' or 'behavioural' level serves to define what will be accepted as evidence of success or failure.

5 OBJECTIVES AND UNIVERSITY TEACHING METHODS

Despite some limitations of the Taxonomy, the work of Bloom and his associates in clarifying objectives served to draw attention to higher level objectives which have often received insufficient attention in university courses and examinations. Undoubtedly the chief limitation is that many important general objectives are not readily fitted into this, or similar hierarchies, although some of them have received attention from other psychologists and from teachers making educational experiments.

One of the most general and all-pervading of objectives neglected in the taxonomies – perhaps because they concentrate on students' performance – is concern for effective use of staff and time. Inevitably this is an objective which underlies the construction of courses and planning of individual sessions of teaching. Experiments in this area have been made to determine what size of class could be taught efficiently at one time in lectures or group discussions, and to compare teaching methods with respect to their demands on the time of teachers. De Cecco (1964) found no difference in capacity to recall information whether students were taught in classes of 18 to 34, or in substantially larger classes of 97 to 127, but the students preferred smaller classes. In an experiment with chemistry tutorials reported by Cottrell (1962) both staff and students preferred smaller discussion groups of 3 and 12 to those of 24 members; but those of 12 proved rather more successful than either smaller groups or larger ones. A saving in time was reported by Erskine and Tomkin (1963) in an experiment substituting two periods of discussion for nine lectures during a three week course of anatomy. In addition students from the experimental group gained more information and were considerably more successful in oral examinations than were those who attended the lectures. Joyce and Weatherall (1957) in comparing different methods of teaching – lectures, discussion groups, practical classes and unsupervised reading – concluded: 'For tutors the size of classes is relevant to the economics of teaching, and the figures amount to 0.05 hours per session per student for lectures (assuming an audience of 60); 0.3 hours per session per student for discussion groups of 12 students, and 0.33 hours per session per student for practical classes on the same scale.... these estimates.... are probably reliable enough to emphasize the economy both to students and staff of lecturing compared with practical classes and discussion groups....'

But this, of course, assumes that each method is used independently. Bligh (1972) cites considerable evidence which suggests that in general a mixture of methods is more effective than any one, on a single occasion. In addition, he has brought together extensive evidence that lectures (as they are normally given) are less effective than other methods if the objective is that students should be stimulated to think or to modify their attitudes. They are, however, as efficient as other methods if the objective is to teach information.

Programmed learning has also been used with the chief aim of economy in teaching time in the Armed Forces. In the Navy (Stavert and Wingate 1966), for example, programmes in basic electronics and basic radio which were illustrated by film course instead of the usual course with the Instruction Officer did better than the conventionally taught groups taking 25 per cent less time in the case of radio teaching. In one experiment in the Army (Wallis 1966) a programme not allowing for practice and repetition proved as effective as a more detailed programme in Automatic Car Transmission System and was completed far more quickly.

Romiszowski (1967) reported that, in industry, education officers found that programmed learning resulted in better retention, faster learning and flexibility in teaching since it could proceed without supervision. Adult students found programmed learning less embarrassing than class teaching because they did not need to admit ignorance in public.

In the university also programmed learning has been proved efficient in a number of instances. Moore (1967) found that group teaching, by a method of pacing, setting a time limit for each pace, resulted in a considerably better speed for slow workers. Times for the machine group were of the order of 30 per cent less than that of slower workers using self-paced books. This saving was effected without significantly affecting the test scores. Biran and Pickering (1968) found that 'unscrambling' a branching programme in genetics and presenting it in linear form decreased learning time without affecting gain in scores. Teather (1968) in listing programmes for teaching undergraduate biology also noted saving of time as an advantage.

As we have seen in discussing schemes of objectives, an activity such as reading the scheme which alerts students to what they should look for in a course makes learning more effective. A number of studies confirm the value of having some kind of 'cognitive map' in advance. A one-week pre-college maths workshop organized by Taylor and Hanson (1969) led to significantly higher grades for those who attended than for controls who were initially rated more able, and their attrition rate was considerably lower. A study by Gardiner, Boddy and Taylor (1969) shows that in teaching applied pharmacology, anaesthesiology and hospital procedure, practical experience in the wards may with advantage be substituted for lectures. Among 74 dental students, the group which spent two days in normal surgical wards – where teaching was minimal but practical experience and contact with all grades of hospital staff were at a maximum – required less time and found it easier to assimilate information than did the group which attended 22 lectures during a period of 10 weeks (Steubner and Johnson 1969). In a recent experiment by Webb (personal communication) a combination of pre-testing with self-marking in a post-test proved highly effective in improving learning, but pre-testing alone made a significant difference.

A dramtic improvement in the ability to make dissections among students of biology has been reported in a personal communication by Goodhue of Trinity College, Dublin, who prepared tapes with diagrams and film-loops to show students how to perform the dissection of a rat, etc. Following study of these aids in place of the usual demonstration, students performed the dissection almost faultlessly in one hour instead of taking the usual three hours and making numerous errors. It would be of interest in this case to investigate what factors were most helpful, eg. the role of coloured diagrams, and to determine what kind of aids would give the necessary skill in a minimum of time or, alternatively, in a manner most likely to transfer to other dissections.

However, despite these evident gains, we shall see that more fundamental objectives in teaching should weigh considerably in the choice of method.

a The development of effective study skills

Study skills include speed and comprehension in reading, use of books and the library and visual aids, the taking of notes, writing of reports, organizing revision and selection of the best methods of study. These skills tend to be taken for granted by many teachers, as though they were unalterable; but where experiments have been made to produce improvements in these respects, considerable gains have been reported. Barclay (1957) used the Harvard films to train a group of adults to read faster and with greater comprehension. The average increase in speed was 81 per cent ranging from 213 per cent to seven per cent. There was an overall improvement in comprehension and, after lectures on methods of skimming and scanning, a cut of about 50 per cent in time to find facts was achieved. Poulton (1961) reviewed a large number of similar experiments with eight different adult populations. All gained considerably in speed and comprehension but, on re-test after an interval, individuals varied greatly in the extent to which they maintained the improvements, some doing so almost completely and others hardly at all. The studies of Jahoda and Thomas (1966) already mentioned may result in similar considerable improvements in strategies of learning while reading.

Attempts to teach study skills by lectures seem usually to have been ineffective but this is to be expected since, like all skills, they need practice and feedback on performance for improvement to be made. Rowntree (1970) recognizes this in his programmed text <u>Learn how to</u>

study in which the reader is required to attempt exercises throughout and receives information as to whether his responses are correct. Active methods are also being used by some librarians to teach use of library facilities. Crossley (1968) reports a higher level of library inquiry and increased use of inter-library services following a short course designed to increase students' skill in searching literature. Bristow (1970) describes a series of seminars in which teachers worked in small groups making book summaries, with the aid of suggestions from the librarian, and subsequently discussed the results. In addition they learned how to organize bibliographies relating to their own special interests.

b Promoting thinking and influencing attitudes

At first sight it may appear that thinking should be classified with cognitive skills rather than with attitudes although we have already drawn attention to an affective element in thinking. That there is an essential difficulty in thinking objectively owing to unconscious assumptions and habits built up in the course of learning has been shown by Abercrombie (1960); reception of information, recollections, observation and description, judgments or inference are alike affected. Abercrombie experimented with undirected group discussions. Her aim was to avoid instruction in a 'correct' method but to develop a scientific method by stimulating students to work out problems among themselves by mutual questioning and correction. For example, in an early study (James, Johnson and Venning 1956), one group of students was trained to be observant in studying X-rays and other visual material, by criticism of their own descriptions and the receipt of visual information. In subsequent comparison of this group with one conventionally taught, in observation of three X-rays, the trained group was superior to a highly significant degree; they made fewer false inferences, fewer inferences unaccompanied by descriptions, more of them considered two hypotheses rather than one only and a smaller number were inappropriately biased by one test in dealing with the succeeding one. Evidently a change in behaviour did occur due to this kind of general discussion.

The influence of discussion on attitudes and thinking has also been shown by Barnett (1958), Hammond and Kern (1959) where the presence or absence of case study discussion proved critical, Lewin (1947), who found that lectures made practically no impression on the behaviour of housewives but that as a result of discussion a substantial number could be persuaded to change their food-habits, and Hallworth (1957) who used interpretation of group discussions to make adult students aware of interactions, hostilities, etc. within the group.

That lectures might have little influence on thinking was suggested further by Elton's comparison of students attending lectures on logic with a group of psychology students; those 'studying' logic made no greater improvement in a reasoning test than did the psychology students (Elton 1965).

Bligh's surveys of comparative studies of teaching methods amply confirm this suspicion; but he suggests ways of modifying the traditional lecture to allow students to play a more active role (1972).

c Oral skills

Oral skills are receiving increasing attention in departments such as engineering where young professional men may be called on to give lucid reports to people with little professional knowledge or to talk impromptu about some possible new project. Both the capacity to put forward a view and understanding of the working of committees are therefore being taught. In departments where students are more specifically training to deal with people such as those of medicine, dentistry and teaching, oral skills have always been emphasized. An inquiry into small group discussion methods in London University by Beard (1967) shows that one objective in their use is the development of skill in reporting to a group or in chairing it.

d Special skills

Within the various university departments many skills peculiar to a field must be learned : for example, in medicine, skills in taking histories, making examinations, making clinical tests, interpretation of symptoms or diagnosis, etc. or in the sciences, skill in handling apparatus in the laboratory, in experimental methods, and so on.

Books are now being produced in which objectives in learning these skills have been analysed in detail. For example, in the book available from BMA by T.S.M. Zorab and the Department of Audio-Visual Communication (1972), the initial learning objectives in the examination of the heart and renal function are listed as follows :

'C Examination of the heart – an aspect of auscultation

The student will be able to

a position both the patient and himself appropriate for cardiac auscultation

b define the proper use of stethoscope's bell and diaphragm

c define a proper stethescope

d define purpose, areas and method of cardiac auscultation

E Quantitative aspect of renal function

The student will be able to calculate renal blood flow from the plasma flow and the haematocrit value in renal arterial blood. '

Korst (1973) spells out objectives for an entire clinical course in considerably less detail and not in behavioural terms, but he introduces a useful innovation by describing four levels of competence, eg. for skills in treating cardiovascular disease, for students :

4.00 Well qualified or very competent

Cardiac resuscitation

Blood pressure determination

Venous and arterial pulse in arms, legs and neck and examination of peripheral vessels

3.00 Familiar with or competent

Chest X-ray interpretation (PA and obliques)

Interpretation of eye grounds in hypertension, etc.

2.00 Awareness or minimal familiarity

Cardiac catheterization and analysis of data, coronory arteriography and other vessel angiography

Pericardiocentesis

Phonocardiography etc.

Korst's lowest level 1.0 Recall of information only is, of course, not relevant in listing skills objectives.

Since it is only five years ago that many teachers of clinical medicine in the UK claimed that it would prove impossible to specify objectives in teaching their subject, this is an impressive advance. Korst's levels of competence might also be applied to teacher training where examination by essay papers are still used extensively. Where this is so, teacher trainers might well ask themselves whether they are not unduly emphasizing the lowest level of competence instead of specifying the skills young teachers need to develop; for instance, in applying psychology in the classroom, or thinking clearly on their own account in addition to repeating the views of a philosopher. If the skills involved were carefully specified – as for the treatment of cardiac arrest – they might be taught more systematically and with greater likelihood of success.

An example of a different kind – the experiment of Goodhue, already mentioned in section I – is relevant. At Guy's Hospital in the Department of Pathology, videotapes of students making physical examinations enable teachers to assess their performance at leisure but they also allow the students to view and to criticize their own performance and thus to improve it. In an experiment in the Physiology Department, students playing the roles of a doctor making tests, the patient and assistant were videotaped and this proved effective in improving students' performance both in making the tests and in communicating more sympathetically with their 'patients'. Role playing of this kind is increasingly used also in courses for General Practitioner Trainers who wish to learn how to teach their trainees more effectively. The trainer and trainee discuss the 'case' and take part in subsequent discussion of the trainer's teaching when the performance is played back on videotape. This is one way to provide practice and feedback on performance which is essential in learning any skill.

e Acquisition of information

In contrast with skills which are learned by practice with feedback, or attitudes which appear to be changed most readily in discussion, information may be committed to memory by a diversity of approaches. Successful experiments in improving immediate recall, or retention, of subject matter are based on what is known of remembering and forgetting in learning. It is known that to assist memory subject matter should be meaningful, inter-relationships between topics should be stressed and frequent short periods should be spent in learning in preference to a few long ones. Forgetting on the other hand, is induced by presenting the learner with many unrelated details, or by interference where a new topic is introduced at the end of a period of study or if two closely similar topics are learned together. To encourage accurate recall, correct responses should be rewarded, or reinforced, immediately, possibly only by knowing that the response is right while wrong responses should be corrected at once, cf. Croxton and Martin (1965), Glynn (1965), Hoare and Inglis (1965), Owen et al. (1965), Stavert and Wingate (1966). Above all, it is important that the student should make a response, overtly if the material is very unfamiliar to him (Leith and Buckle 1966); to be efficient his learning must actively employ his ability to organize new information into his existing mental schemata (Holland et al. 1966). Where learning takes place by rote, with little understanding, subsequent forgetting is rapid.

In using audio-visual techniques, recall is more efficient if repetition is possible (Holloway 1964), if more than one method is used (Vernon 1946), and if interference from note taking is avoided (Ash and Carlton 1953).

An experiment by Elley (1966) suggests that making errors while learning has an adverse effect on recall of rote-learned material but does not affect the recall of meaningful material. He points out that in preparing programmed texts for students there is no need to be restricted by the assumption that errors should be kept to a minimum. We have already noted evidence of the value of alerting the learner to what to look for before he reads or listens to a lecture.

A point which teachers often do not appreciate adequately is that it is equally or more efficient to give a clear outline in a text or lecture than to give considerable detail – probably because detail tends to confuse the learner. Experiments in the RAF show that, students using programmed learning over a period of weeks took considerably less time, particularly in the case of those using a programme reduced to essentials (Wallis et al. 1969). A similar effect was found in a course for medical science personnel who attempted programmes having five differing amounts of redundancy (Valverdi and Morgan 1970); it was the leanest programme which proved most efficient.

f Higher cognitive skills

Very few experiments have been made into the teaching of more complex mental abilities. Hayes (1964), who studied the student dissertation reported that over a three year period there was a definite improvement in the handling of bibliographical materials. There was increased student participation in research and in the student research journal, 25 per cent of papers in 1961, 26.5 per cent in 1962 and 45.5 per cent in 1963 were based on original work. Collier (1966) used work in co-operative groups to encourage critical thinking and to overcome the habit of accepting and memorizing instruction. As with other skills, it seems that the higher verbal abilities and skills are developed by practice together with criticism.

A different approach to the realization of cognitive objectives has been made by Gagné (1965) and other associationists who have broken down subject matter into its constituent skills in order to recommend teaching methods appropriate to each one. Thus, if the aim is that of making multiple discriminations such as distinctions between terms, or formulae, it is imperative that the items to be distinguished should be well learned individually and that the tendency of interference between them should be overcome by repetition of the correct associations, or chains of associations, for each item. It is then possible to bring them together to distinguish them with a minimum of interference. In learning concepts, on the other hand, bringing together a number of instances of the class, relationship, property or abstraction may suffice for the student to see what it is that they have in common; but he will also need to learn to discriminate negative instances and will almost certainly be aided by verbal description and he will find it essential in the case of abstract concepts. At the next level of complexity, simple principles combine concepts as in 'masses attract one another'; but, in higher level principles, simpler principles may themselves be seen in relation to each other as in 'the force of attraction between two bodies is inversely proportional to their distance'. Organized knowledge consists of many such interrelationships. Successful learning, therefore, depends on the fundamentals being secure and lower-level principles well known, before the higher level ones are introduced. But in general, higher level learning of concepts and principles is very well retained, in contrast with associations and discriminations.

The highest cognitive objective discussed by Gagné is that of problem solving. To find a solution the student must know his goal and then select and use appropriate principles to achieve it. Katona (1940) has shown that presenting solutions for students to learn is markedly ineffective in teaching problem solving. It is somewhat more effective to state principles which could be used; but a method of guided discovery which does not mention the principle and leads the student, by questions, to 'discover' it for himself is the most effective of all. Maier (1930) found that giving instructions which recalled known principles assisted his subjects in solving problems. These findings may account for a difference noted by Beard (1967) that mathematicians using small group discussions to ensure that students understood principles seemed more satisfied with the method than those who used these methods to work through specific problems.

In a recent study of problem solving in physics, students at an Australian university (Connor 1967) found great difficulty in dealing with unfamiliar types of problem and attempted to use deductive processes even when these were inappropriate. The writer suggests that thinking in problem solving should be made more explicit in a conscious attempt to improve it and that flexibility and inventiveness should be demanded of students in university courses. In England, this is already happening. At Imperial College and the City University for example, in new laboratory courses, students are required to solve problems of an unfamiliar kind even though they may initially lack a knowledge of the relevant theory.

Chapter 4

ARE OBJECTIVES REALIZED? EVALUATION OF LEARNING AND TEACHING

Ruth M. Beard

THE FUNCTION OF EVALUATION

Evaluation in the higher stages of education has two main functions - award of qualifications such as A levels, diplomas and degrees which serve as entry to other courses or to professions, and provisions of information or feedback as to the success of learning and teaching. Traditionally, considerable attention has been given to the former, whereas the latter has been left to the devices of teachers and students who have often provided or obtained information too late to make learning more effective. For many years proposals for reform have been in terms of adjustments to the examination system or demand for better selection. Extensive researches were set up to relate students' performance at entry with their achievement in finals, usually with no reference to the organization of courses or to the teaching which came between. It was hardly surprising if they ended in selecting good examinees among the less able students. Even today, it is the abilities of the students, rather than the quality of teaching and learning in a school, which are criticized when students fail; interestingly, when students do well their teachers are commonly given the credit by their colleagues - it is the teachers of other schools who point to the exceptional calibre of the students!

The more recent concern with the systematic study of teaching and stress on educational technology promises to place the emphasis where it should be : on the improvement of learning. Moreover, teachers and psychologists who have studied examining techniques point out that to include all the skills and abilities which should be tested and to arrive at more reliable assessments requires substantial changes in examinations. Although in the long term this must involve acquisition of qualifications, there is no reason why a qualification should be given for performance in examinations taken on one occasion, or within a short interval. On the contrary, evidence accumulates to suggest that in evaluating skills, for instance, some form of continuous assessment is more satisfactory. Intermediate objectives may still be assessed by performance in tests, projects, essays, reports on a series of experiments etc. and these are adequately provided in many departments. But evaluation of short term objectives – which contributes mainly feedback to the students – is often insufficient. Students need immediate comments on performance of skills, questions which will enable them to assess their understanding of current work or ability to apply content of an informative lecture, discussion of experiments they have performed or problems they have failed to solve, and so on. Since teaching time is limited, aids to learning such as these need to be of a kind which enable students to correct their own performance, wherever possible, or have it corrected by machine or unskilled helpers.

Undoubtedly, the teacher himself needs more evaluation of his performance than he has formerly had. Various methods of obtaining useful information are being explored by employing modern audio-visual techniques, or by consultation with the students. For example, use of videotape enables the lecturer to see himself in action and so to monitor his own performance, whilst students' opinions on teaching may be obtained by use of questionnaires. In these ways, it is hoped that teachers will be enabled to give maximum help to their students and, possibly, to channel their efforts into the teaching skills which they perform best.

TECHNIQUES IN EXAMINING AND TESTING

Since space does not permit us to take a sample course, to break it down into objectives and to indicate how we consider the attainments of each objective might be evaluated, the reader is recommended to study the schemes already referred to earlier in the text: in Physics (Pole 1973), physiology (Naeraa 1972), design (Piper 1967), the training of biology teachers (Dallas and Piper 1973) some illustrative examples are given in the appendix. In this chapter we shall discuss various evaluative techniques noting which kinds of objectives each is most suited to assess. Claims for each technique and criticisms arising from research will be briefly discussed and references will be given to more extensive research findings.

a <u>Essay writing</u>

Criticisms of essay examinations are usually advanced on the grounds of unreliable marking and consequent difficulty in making fair assessments of students. A less frequently mentioned criticism is that they may be used where essay writing is irrelevant, in assessing skills which are mainly practical, for example. Beard, Levy and Maddox (1964) observed the high correlations between scores in a test of verbal ability and examination scores in dynamics, engineering drawing and 'strength of materials' in an engineering department at Birmingham and questioned whether perhaps the examinations were too verbal for the skills they were intended to evaluate. Certainly there are departments which use essays as an examination technique in finals although none have been written throughout the preceding three-year course! This suggests that a serious review of objectives should be undertaken to ensure that the form of the final assessment is fully relevant to what students are supposed to learn in such courses.

Considerable evidence has been collected which shows that the marking of essays tends to be unreliable : examiners often differ substantially from each other in the marks they assign, and even the same examiner may differ significantly in the marks he gives to the same set of essays on two occasions. Much of the evidence is surveyed by Cox in the Universities Quarterly of June (1967) and by Beard in the Report of the Universities Spring Conference 1969 convened by the Committee of Vice-Chancellors and Principals and the Association of University Teachers (1969). To give but one example : Bull (1956) calculated correlations for two examiners with themselves in marking a set of essays on fairly factual medical subjects and found them as low as 0.28 and 0.42. The mean marks given by the two examiners correlated 0.34 with each other. In other words a chance assignment of marks would have been almost as effective a means of assessment. He concluded that the essay paper of the kind in which four questions were to be answered in three hours was very inefficient in distinguishing between students.

Those who value essay examinations have sought ways of arriving at more consistent standards of marking. Bull (1956) found that greater reliability could be obtained by using more examiners and averaging their marks for each paper. The mean marks of four independent examiners used in this way raised the consistency to 0.9. Although there is an advantage in a plurality of markers, there are two objections to this method: there is not usually a sufficiency of examiners to have every essay marked independently four times, and averaging marks can obscure those interesting cases where examiners have difficulty in agreeing and which probably, therefore, deserve individual discussion. Another alternative which is increasingly used in arts departments is to assess several of a student's essays, counting the average grade towards his final assessment. Thus, in York, one of five methods of assessment in English allows students to enter their five best tutorial essays (essays revised after discussion with the tutor), for evaluation, three of these are assessed independently by four examiners who study the remaining two essays only in the event of disagreement (Brockbank 1968, Jones 1969).

For different reasons other modifications in essay examinations have been proposed. Jones (1969) reports that three-hour examinations, with textbooks and dictionaries allowed, test ability to work against the clock. A paper of stated length prepared over 14 days allows unrestricted use of books and makes demands on students such as any author may experience. Long essays, used to allow students to write about their optional topic, give students opportunity to make significant and fresh discoveries whilst working in a chosen field. Thus each examination method is used to test achievement of different objectives, although neither Brockbank nor Jones has analysed the course in any of the ways described in this volume. In other departments announcement of the topic in advance has become common practice; thus students arrive prepared at the examination. In a department of biochemistry one of four methods of examining allows students six weeks to prepare for an essay examination on a topic of their choice. (Beard and Pole 1971). In this instance a main objective is that students should learn to obtain information for themselves, through use of books and libraries or in discussion with their peers. Some teachers who have used the method, report that time to prepare results in generally better performance but that the rank order of the students remains much the same. An increased time allowance may be needed to overcome the problem of a student who thinks profoundly but rather slowly. Amongst the diversity of methods used at York, Brockbank (1968) found that about two thirds of the students did equally well whatever method was used, one sixth each did better in papers written at leisure or in traditional papers, whilst one tenth of these did either better or worse in examinations than by continuous assessment.

Although the variation in standard between examiners is greater in some subjects than in others, and may be slight where teachers from one school mark the papers, for they are likely to share similar views of both subject and students, nevertheless it seems that much of the confidence expressed in existing essay examinations is misplaced. Even where teachers agree closely this may arise less from common objectivity than from a shared bias such as the 'halo-effect', for example. As early as the 1920's it was recognized that teachers tend to rate highly all performances of students they agree to be 'good' whereas they tend to give low marks to students who are considered 'poor' (Woodworth 1922). Tales of students who exchanged essays written in term time and found that each, nevertheless, received his customary 'A' or 'C' are not wholly without foundation. Internal marking in finals tends to confirm such biases.

Attempts to agree on a marking system assigning marks for particular information, for knowledge of principles, etc. and with an agreed bonus for originality go some way to producing greater consistency when candidates all attempt the same questions. Stalnaker (1951), who used such a method in marking school essays, achieved a correlation between markers of 0.85; but when questions were longer and more involved, as is commonly the case in higher education, consistency dropped to 0.58. However, it seems probable that one cause of inconsistency is that teachers do not observe the same errors or, in marking the same paper twice, that a single examiner changes his criteria, for instance, emphasizing knowledge and use of information on one occasion and style on another. In addition in discussing the evaluation of communication skills, Palmer (1961), suggests that the evaluation of writing is difficult unless the topic assigned is well focussed and its purpose is clear to both students and instructors. He also points out the value of obtaining a number of assessments of skill in writing since a student will like some topics and be better informed about them than others, and variations in mood will affect his performance.

As a method of learning, however, it is generally agreed that essay writing is effective, and for this reason, if for no other, it would perhaps be unwise to exclude it from examinations for there is a tendency among students to judge unimportant what is not examined. Simply to write an essay on a well-chosen topic obliges the student to collect information, to organize it, to weigh evidence for different views and to find words in which to express them. Even when little criticism is given this is likely to assist clarity in thinking; but if, in addition, it receives the kind of detailed criticism which is realized in an ideal tutorial it will lead to the student becoming aware of his misconceptions and limitations and so lead him to greater objectivity and breadth in thinking. Since the ratio of staff to students does not allow frequent tutorials in the majority of colleges, there is a tendency to give uninformative grades. This can be avoided without excessive labour if teachers devise a scheme enabling them to write detailed criticisms on each student's essay, perhaps in the form of agreed symbols, or if they take a few essays from time to time, analyse their content, and make clear their merits and defects for the benefit of an entire group. In this way, students receive information as to their performance and guidance for future improvement. As Palmer (1961) points out, in marking an essay on, say, the causes of Babbitt's rebellion, a grade of F might mean that the mechanics were so bad that the paper was not acceptable; it might mean that the student was inaccurate in his references to a book even though his evaluation of the reasons for the rebellion was extremely good; it might mean that his references to the book, although accurate, had little to do with the problem. If the student is to improve, therefore, he must be provided with a clear indication of how to do so. Examples of tutor's marking in a publication of the Open University show that this can be done both informatively and succinctly.

On balance, therefore, the essay appears capable of making a valuable contribution to the student's thinking and capacity to arrange his ideas but a cumulative assessment of the student's essays over a period of time might well be more reliable than the results of essay examinations.

b <u>Objective tests</u>

The type of examination most favoured as an alternative to essay examinations is the multiple-choice objective test. When first devised these tests tended to be limited to items requiring merely recall or recognition of information and, in consequence, there was considerable antagonism to their introduction in higher education in England. Now that they are in limited use, antagonism is sometimes aroused on the part of students in departments which frequently employ objective tests requiring only recall of factual material. Perhaps the main reason for their indignation is that they know that tests are now available which require thought about the subject, in determining how to apply it, or in working out the solution to a problem.

Educational taxonomies have been employed to decide on suitable categories of cognitive skills before the tests are prepared. In an investigation into an existing multiple-choice examination in 1961, McGuire (1963) decided on an eight-level classification: recall of specific facts, abstraction of principles, selection of appropriate generalizations to explain phenomena, interpretation of data presented in a variety of forms, application of principles to solution of problems of a familiar type, analysis of unfamiliar constellations of events, evaluation of a total situation and synthesis of data into new and meaningful wholes. At that time she found that some 78 per cent of the items in National Board medical examinations fell into the lowest category of 'isolated recall', five per cent required recognition of meaning of a fact or concept, 11 per cent involved ability to generalize, leaving seven per cent only in the remaining five categories, of which 'unfamiliar applications' and 'ability to synthesize' remained unrepresented.

Today anyone undertaking to prepare such a test decides on his categories in advance assigning to them agreed numbers of items within each topic. For an A-level physics test devised at the Institute of Educational Technology in the University of Surrey, the following grid was prepared:

	Knowledge	Comprehension	Application	Analysis/ evaluation	Total
Gen. Physics					15
Heat					11
Light					11
Sound					8
Elec. and Mag.					22
Atomic Phys.					8
Total	19	34	15	7	75

From the totals it is possible to work out approximate numbers of items to be devised in each category. Thus in Atomic Physics, $19 \times 8 \div 75$, ie. approximately two of the total 75 items should come in the 'knowledge' category. This category is sometimes criticized because it contains so wide a range of knowledge – from specific facts to extensive bodies of knowledge. Nedelsky (1949) proposed subdividing it into three sub-classes – subject matter knowledge, analytical knowledge, and knowledge of methodology. The first of these corresponds roughly with 'knowledge of specific facts'. The second is described as 'knowledge of relations and patterns'. The third is also concerned with apprehension of relationships, in particular the inter-relation of different areas of physics and between physics and other sciences.

Items themselves may take a variety of forms. Those most favoured offer four or five choices to the examinee, providing plausible alternatives to a correct answer or asking the student to find an exception, eg.

> 'All of the following are factors known to upset the Hardy-Weinberg Law (of genetic equilibrium) EXCEPT
>
> A population size
> B natural selection
> C random reproduction
> D genetic drift
> E migration'

The normal criticism of this type of item is that it is possible for the student to guess a proportion of answers correctly and that, if the options are not very carefully prepared, there may be cues to wrong ones (for example, if they are too sweeping in asserting 'all....', 'always....', 'never....', etc.) or to the correct one if it is conspicuously more carefully phrased than the others. However, these are avoidable features of test items and guessing can be penalized by subtracting a proportion of the score for wrong answers if this is felt to be desirable.

Although the difficulty level of the majority of items in tests is not high, their difficulty should be determined in accordance with the aims of the test. The form of the question can be altered to make it more complex – and to add to the odds against guessing correctly – by a series of cross matching statements. For example, the following item suggested by Bloom and his associates (1954), in the category of application, would give occasion for some hard thinking at least to weaker students in elementary astronomy:

> 'You have acquired some knowledge of the earth and its motions as they really exist. In this exercise you are to identify the effects of some wholly imaginary conditions. After each item number on the answer sheet underline the appropriate letter:
>
> A- if the item would be true if the earth were <u>not</u> inclined on on its axis

B- if the item would be true if the orbit of the earth were a circle rather than an ellipse

C- if the item would be true if the earth revolved toward the west rather than toward the east

D- if the item would be true if the earth had half its present diameter but retained its general mass

E- if the item would be true if the earth had no moon

Assume only one of the above imaginary conditions occurs at a time.

1 All the solar days would be of equal length.

2 Objects would weigh four times as much as they do now.

3 The celestial equator and the ecliptic would be identical.

4 The sun would set in the east.

5 A different North Star would need to be chosen.

6 The force of gravity would be four times as great.

7 The orbital speed of the earth would not vary during the year.

8 We would know less about the nature of the sun.

9 Night and day would be of equal length in all latitudes all year long. '

The kind of item which invites the examinee to relate categories reduces the possibility of guessing eg. 'cross link the following:

man	leptospirosis
cattle	shigellosis
earthworm	yellow fever
rodents	Q. fever
birds	galloping ear rot (ascariasis) etc. '

Whilst an item which requires recognition of more difficult relationships may demand careful thinking to arrive at the correct answer:

> 'Either of the two statements of each of the following sentences is true or false and, if both are true, may be related to cause and effect. Identify your answer for each one by one of the letters in the left-hand column.
>
> | Answer | First statement | Second statement | Related |
> | --- | --- | --- | --- |
> | A | True | True | Yes |
> | B | True | True | No |
> | C | True | False | - |
> | D | False | True | - |
> | E | False | False | - |
>
> Sentence
>
> 1 Mersatyl produces a metabolic acidosis BECAUSE of the loss of alkali in the urine.'

Berg gives examples suitable for use in teaching and testing social sciences and history. (Dressel <u>et al</u>. 1961).

It must be evident, even to those who have not attempted it, that the chief expenditure of time in preparing these tests is in designing promising questions whereas the selection of items and their marking can be at least partly achieved by computer methods; the latter may be done by machine for large numbers of candidates, or very rapidly, by someone unskilled, for smaller groups. To reduce time in setting them, co-operative efforts are desirable. When a 'bank' of several thousand suitable items has been collected it is possible to feed data to a computer and to programme it to select alternative tests of given difficulty levels, covering stated topics and categories of cognitive abilities; even the reliability of the test can be specified once the items have been adequately tried out among a population comparable with that to be tested and norms can be computed.

Further advantages of these tests are that results can be obtained rapidly – students receive their grading on the same, or the next day, in time to revise for a further test if necessary. Moreover, although it is usually agreed that the 'bank' of questions must not be circulated, similar items serve to make very effective tests for revision or for testing at the end of a lecture or short course. Since there is little to write, a large number of items can be answered in a very few minutes. At Surrey, for example, lecture notes and multiple-choice tests with answers are circulated simultaneously.

Currently, in America, attention is being given to the development of new types of objective examinations to test higher cognitive skills. In the medical field, where considerable progress has been made, the tests require the students to interpret information or to make judgments of the kind they would have to make as physicians (Beard 1967). As with other objective tests, when an item analysis is made, it is easy to identify specific strengths and weaknesses of individuals and to follow progress over a period of time or as a result of curriculum changes. Initially, at least, the help of a psychologist or a specialist in education is likely to be needed in devising and marking more complex objective tests.

c <u>Short answer tests</u>

The short answer test has the advantage of requiring recall rather than recognition of a correct answer and so is well suited where information must be known. Such questions may consist in giving definitions of terms, making labelled diagrams with brief notes, providing lists, for example, of procedures in dealing with a technical fault or reasons in order of preference for choice of a medical treatment. Some attempt may also be made to combine the merits of essay writing with those of brevity and the objectivity of multiple-choice tests. For example, medical students may be asked to answer a multiple-choice question putting in order the steps in the aetiology of a condition, and then to outline briefly its treatment. Or a brief description in a few lines, of essential features may be asked for. This has the merit that the student must show some ability in organizing information, but the brevity of the answer allows for a comparatively simple and objective scheme of marking. In the physics department at Rhodes University South Africa, items of this kind are used in tests and examinations, chiefly for the younger students. For instance:

> 'Monochromatic light from two parallel narrow slits separated by 1 mm. falls onto a screen 50 cm. away. The interference fringes produced are separated by 0.25 mm.

a What is the wave length of the light?

b What is the frequency of the light?

c Describe all the changes that would occur in the pattern if

i the spacing between the slits was slowly decreased

ii the wavelength of the light was slowly decreased

iii the slit widths were slowly decreased

Draw sketches if necessary.'

Since these questions are more difficult to mark than multiple-choice items (at least until computers acquire ability to read) they are less in use. But, because they are easier to prepare, and require recall, or thinking, on the part of the examinee rather than mere recognition of a right answer, they may often be preferable to multiple-choice tests.

d Oral examinations

Oral examinations have been the traditional method of examining in some European countries; but to provide as many as six (or even more) examiners and to ask candidates sufficient questions, or sufficiently searching ones, to test their knowledge is too time consuming where the number of candidates is large. However, since an engineer, for example, will often need to give verbal explanations of his plans and to defend them in argument, there is a case for emphasizing verbal skills in teaching and examining.

Like essays, however, oral questions tend to be an unreliable method of examining. Bull (1956) found that, in oral medical examinations, agreement between two examiners testing the same candidate on the same patient was good but became somewhat less so when candidates were tested with different patients. The candidates' volubility has been shown to influence results (Evans, Ingersoll and Smith 1966) and in an American study of oral examinations, grading became less stringent during the course of each day's examining and also on each succeeding examination day (Cotton and Petersen 1967). Reliability varied greatly between different teams of examiners and within teams. The oral examination has the disadvantage, also, that a clash of personalities between examiners, or between examiner and student may influence results. One external examiner reported recently that as a student entered the room the internal examiner remarked audibly 'This one needs taking down a peg'. The external examiner compensated for this initial disadvantage to the student by asking easy questions only, but was involved subsequently in a long argument with the internal examiner. In such a case one sees the need for the large number of examiners sometimes used in European oral examinations; but it seems probable that factors other than skill in the subject such as the 'halo-effect' and verbal fluency play a part in any oral examination.

In the English Department at York (Jones 1969) a form of viva is employed as part of the assessment. Oral contributions to seminars and tutorials are assessed continuously throughout the term. Each seminar is conducted by two tutors, which allows one to take initiative in guiding discussion whilst the other operates mainly as an observer. The effect of this on performance in seminars seems to be entirely good.

New techniques offer to make oral examining more objective now that, in certain cases, a permament record can be obtained on tape or videotape. Discussion between a linguist and the examiner, or a medical student taking a history from a patient, can be recorded and examined again at leisure. In either of these cases, the record can also be used to demonstrate his own faults to the student; for, like most good methods of examining, it is also a valuable aid to teaching. To increase objectivity in evaluating the student's performance, an analysis of the behaviours the student should demonstrate needs to be undertaken beforehand so that each one can be assessed separately. In this way, the danger of influence from 'halo-effect' which is at a maximum in an overall, unanalysed judgment, is at least reduced.

e Examining practical skills

The examination of practical skills is a prime concern of dental and design departments and, to a lesser degree, of medical schools. It may also be of some importance in the assessment of scientific experiments. Although in industry the teaching of practical skills, and their evaluation, has received considerable attention, no detailed analyses of skills in university teaching have been reported. There are, of course, two types of skill : those to which knowledge of results is automatic or 'intrinsic' and those in which some additional 'intrinsic' information must be supplied by an instructor. In the former, even the beginner can see, or feel, that something has gone correctly into an assembly, or is wrongly placed, etc. but in the latter, as when a medical student begins to make physical examination, he needs advice on what to feel for, how to place his hands, etc. and would be unable to learn without it. Thus the student can assess his own skill in the former case but an instructor or examiner is necessary in the second.

The extent to which examiners may differ in marking practical work is illustrated by an investigation into the marking of 14 clinical medical examinations. Candidates needed to be in the top third to be reasonably certain to be passed by all of them; 15 candidates were failed by at least one examiner but none was failed by all examiners (Wilson et al. 1969). However, reasons for these differences were not investigated.

It seems probable that new techniques will assist also in assessing skills. Videotape, for example, allows the student to see his own performance or the examiner to view it again. Experiments in some London hospitals suggest that this is of greatest value to the student, but a collection of permanent records will also serve as a basis for analysis of skills, or of errors while learning them, which should lead both to more rapid learning and to increasingly accurate assessments.

In the case of arts subjects where examiners may be expected to differ even more widely, Popham (1972) suggests that independent judges might use the method of comparing and rating performances of a student at the beginning and end of a course (eg. in ability to prepare watercolour prints). In this way students might be given approximate grades and, incidentally, a measure of the effectiveness of the course could be obtained.

f Problems, experiments and projects

Solutions to problems and ability to perform experiments have always been an essential part of mathematical and scientific examinations; yet, if a university teacher seeks for even a single publication in Britain to assist him in setting better problem papers or in assessing experimental work more objectively he will do so in vain. No-one has prepared categories, such as Bloom's, analysing the skills required in solving problems; but this is needed in order to set well balanced papers drawing on a variety of such skills, rather than almost exclusively on low-level ones, or those which happen to interest individual examiners on one occasion. In some ways, examinations consisting of problems and experiments should be the easiest to assess since the test is whether the candidate solves the problems or completes the experiment successfully. But in mathematics examinations there is evidence that students' performances in successive sets of paper may vary considerably. For example, Dale (1959) reports of candidates who failed an examination in June with marks of 27, 25, 32 and 36, that in September they received 58, 63, 59 and 76 respectively, while the marks of one student varied from fail to first-class standard in a series of examinations. This may well be because different skills are required to a greater or lesser degree on different occasions. Until skills in problem solving have been analysed and identified there seems little hope of any substantial improvement in either teaching or examining it.

Introduction of open-ended experiments and projects adds further difficulties to applying traditional kinds of evaluation. Since examining is rather unreliable even when students perform the same experiments, it is inevitable that when they perform different experiments, write on different topics or justifiably reach different conclusions in an open-ended experiment, evaluation on a common basis is almost impossible. In chapter 1, however, we considered the analysis of an industrial design course into objectives to be attained at different stages of the course or within different projects. This is, at the moment, the most promising way of establishing common criteria in creative work and points to the need for teachers in higher education to specify their objectives in teaching with much greater precision. A series of assessments for each student also overcomes to some extent the unreliability of giving a final grade for a single piece of work.

CONTINUOUS ASSESSMENT

The term 'continuous assessment' may be used either of assessment designed for the benefit of the learner who continuously gets feedback on his success in learning, or of a system of testing and grading designed for the information of teachers. In the former case, it may take the form of programmed learning, test questions on topics recently learned, discussion following questions, fairly detailed criticism of experimental work, reports or essays, etc. In the latter, it is more likely to consist of tests every few weeks which are intended to have a motivating effect on students – since failure to work will be demonstrated, and abler students, at least, compete for high positions. Either kind of assessment may – but need not – give some indication as to the effectiveness of teaching.

In some subjects it is possible to plan periods of teaching so that learning is evaluated. One method, originally tried out in a post-graduate medical course (Mosel 1964), has since been used in London with good effect. This consists in giving a shortened, well planned lecture, stressing principles, before setting a few questions or problems which students answer individually; these are then discussed between neighbours, differences being resolved by looking up points or in argument. Finally, any outstanding difficulties are put to the lecturer. There are several advantages to such a method: firstly, the normal period of one hour for a lecture has been found too long for students to give their full attention (McLeish 1966); secondly, many psychologists have shown that any method which involves the active response of the learner results in more effective learning and, thirdly, by joining different groups, the teacher can discover for himself what students find difficult to follow. In this way learning and evaluation proceed hand in hand. Bligh outlines a number of such methods in his book What's the use of lectures? (1971).

The development of computer-assisted teaching increases the possibility of giving feedback to the learner and responding to his particular skills or difficulties. Since it is even more adaptable than programmed books and teaching machines it should lead, like testing in teaching, to highly effective learning. For it has access to an amount of information which would be excessive for any one teacher to recall, and on this very broad basis of accumulated 'experience' can make 'decisions' as to the appropriate further route in learning for each student. However, it remains to see how long students will be interested to learn in so impersonal a manner and whether some types of students – perhaps the most creative ones – will prefer to follow their own devices. Even without this development it seems likely that undue emphasis on individual work throughout our secondary and tertiary systems loses much of the value of argument between equals and therefore, of the learning which takes place during discussions between students.

The alternative, or additional, policy of employing kinds of continuous assessment, consisting of tests where the students are given the results but do not know their errors promptly, has less to recommend it. Although this puts students under pressure to work hard and to make constant revision, tests are liable to arouse excessive anxiety in a few students and may encourage an attitude of 'getting by' or studying how to obtain good grades rather than to master the subject. However, the 'cheerful extroverts' among students may require such a stimulus to make them work; usually only the introverts become excessively anxious. It is, therefore, for the teacher to judge the personality type of his students and to use frequent tests which are graded if this seems desirable.

Both teaching staff and students have mixed attitudes to assessment of course work as part of a yearly grade or final qualification. Those who argue in favour of it perhaps have in mind that work should proceed by the first kind of continuous assessment. Teaching staff against it tend to feel that course work is often not the unaided work of the student and that this kind of assessment is, therefore, unreliable, while students opposed to the inclusion of marks for course work in final grades point to the low marks some teachers habitually give or to cases where student and teacher are at loggerheads and low marks are given deliberately by an offended member of staff. However, such difficulties do not always apply and, if continuous assessment is felt to be important – as in teaching skills, problems of uneven or unfair marking may be overcome by requiring more than one member of staff to make assessments. Meanwhile, where course marks are allowed in a final assessment, they normally count for a small proportion of the total marks. Until more objective methods of assessing learning and performance are available, perhaps via computers, it seems desirable to use course work to provide feedback on learning. If it is employed for purposes of evaluation for qualifications its shortcomings need to be borne in mind.

EVALUATION OF TEACHING

The evaluation of teaching presents many problems since individuals differ in their performance on different occasions, with different groups of students, and in teaching different topics; but to provide feedback on specific performances is a simpler matter and is likely to have an immediate beneficial effect on teaching.

In London University several methods are fairly commonly in use. A number of lecturers make a habit of taping their sessions of teaching and listening to them subsequently. They report that this helps them to be critical of their delivery of lectures, the kinds of questions they ask or comments they offer in discussion, etc. A few lecturers, in addition, invite colleagues to attend their sessions of teaching and to offer their criticisms. The most effective method, so far, however, seems to be the use of a questionnaire such as that prepared by teachers from nine science departments (Beard 1968); this is designed for students to fill in their comments on a particular session of teaching early in a course. Main headings refer to extraneous factors such as noise, temperature, etc., delivery of the lecture, its content and organization, and the use of visual aids. Since this kind of evaluation takes place early in a course, it is possible to modify teaching in good time to meet students' difficulties. All the students have to do is to underline one of five comments such as :

Material very clearly and attractively presented	Material well presented	Satisfactory	Untidy. Rather crowded. Partly illegible	Far too crowded. Illegible

but space is provided for additional comments and this is normally used. Teachers say that their students take the request for their views very seriously; those who have reported, in detail, mention comments on unsuspected inaudibility at the periphery of a lecture room, requests for more illustrations, for more applications of theory, or for a slower pace when notes must be taken; students of electrical engineering stated a preference for circuit diagrams in colour rather than in black and white. Response to these comments and requests has resulted not only in more effective teaching but in much improved rapport with classes. Even where teachers believed that staff-student relations were already very good some have been surprised at the difference made by the use of the questionnaire. They comment on unexpectedly better co-operation from their students who converse with them more freely and become more obviously interested in their sessions of teaching.

Other methods of evaluation arise from the use of new techniques. Most valuable is the careful analysis of objectives in teaching, such as that which is undertaken in preparing programmed books, for this draws attention to points which may previously have been neglected. Everyone who breaks down a topic into its successive objectives – putting it into the best order for students to follow and writing frames which will enable them to work quite independently – discovers how much he has been accustomed to taking for granted in talking to a class, either as to their knowledge or data which they can manage without. Some teachers who have progressed no further than this in writing programmes report that the exercise has radically altered their approach to testing.

Objective tests and examinations should also provide evaluation of teaching if detailed results are available to teachers. In this way it is possible for a teacher to find out how well students answered questions relating to subjects he taught them. It is astonishing that it is not universal practice to make results available to teachers; yet on the contrary, it is sometimes impossible for teachers to obtain them even though they wish to.

One way to obtain immediate information as to students' understanding of a topic is to ask multiple-choice questions in a feedback classroom. At the Royal Veterinary College, for example, an electrical system has been devised so that when students select one of four buttons to press on their desks their choices are shown on a panel on the lecturer's desk. This enables him to see whether they know the correct answer or what proportions choose different erroneous answers.

The use of television and videotape has scarcely been tried but it has obvious value in allowing a teacher to see how he looks in front of his class and whether he is making sufficient contact with them. Perhaps the use of two-way television (in an experiment by R.F. Mager reported by a visiting scholar) in which students worked in cubicles and could turn off the teacher when they wished would be beneficial in training. Mager found that teachers explained points at too great length so that students lost patience yet the teachers continued their explanations to the end even when students had switched off!

A further possibility of new techniques in training was explored by Kersch (1962) who used film or still pictures and a sound track of sixty classroom situations during the first three days of student training. Student teachers were required to behave to the screen as they would to the class, pictures and sound volume being changed in accordance with their behaviour. In this way, Hawaiian student teachers who normally speak too softly were rapidly trained to raise their voices, and other desirable behaviours were fairly quickly induced. Small, still pictures proved more effective than moving, life-size ones, perhaps because there was less to take in at once. Possibly the 'treatment' for a new university teacher who spoke too quietly or dully would be to see pictures of the 'class' walking out, whereas if he was interesting and lucid successive pictures would show the class increasingly attentive and enthusiastic; but so far this method of supplying continuous feedback to the teacher in training has not been tried in Britain.

EVALUATION OF COURSES AND INNOVATIONS

In normal circumstances in colleges and universities there are few attempts to evaluate courses except through impressions teachers gain of their students' interest and prowess. Evaluation procedures are considered important only in the case of new courses, or where a programme of courses is introduced and the financing body, or its organizers, wish to know whether it achieves the purposes for which it was set up. At one level, therefore, evaluation is concerned with achievement of objectives and whether methods used are the most effective for their purpose. At another level, the whole concept of courses may be challenged, as for instance in the case of refresher courses for clinical doctors some of whom claim that informal lunch-time meetings are more effective. If this is so, rethinking of basic assumptions may be called for. Or the organizers may be concerned with the responses of course members, their continuing interest and quality of activity in the field. Alternatively, their chief concern may be with various consequences – including unexpected ones – of the innovatory procedures.

Inevitably, therefore, evaluation may take a diversity of forms. Methods most commonly employed are study of students' results in examinations and tests, their performance in course work such as essays, use of student opinion given in discussion or on questionnaires, teachers' impressions of students' performance and interest, or employment of methods in teaching and learning which provide feedback both to students and their teachers.

Currently there is a movement towards giving more weight to students' developing interests and to behavioural changes than to gain in information or examination performance. Gauvain (1968), for instance, observes that measurement by examination success may not adequately measure the achievement of the aims of the course if these are to change the students' approach to the subject studied, especially if the examination is set by external assessors unfamiliar with these aims. She notes too that failure may be particularly damaging to postgraduates, especially those from overseas who may be denied opportunity to attempt the examination a second time. She suggests that a fairer judgment of attainment can probably be made by an internal examination which includes assessment of classwork, as this allows measurement both of change in outlook and change in real knowledge. In addition, she gives particular attention to student opinion on the organization, content and methods of instruction.

In the light of the preceding considerations, the recent claim of Parlett and Hamilton (1972) that measurement of performance before and after a course should be rejected in favour of a study of the wider contexts in which the course operates seems not wholly realistic; but their purpose to some extent differs from that of teachers and certain traditional research workers. Instead of setting up criteria of effectiveness, and attempting to measure how far a new method achieves them, they aim to help the innovator to identify those procedures and elements in an innovatory educational process which seem to have desirable results, whether these were intended or not. In consequence their activities may result in redirection of the programme and modification of its aims as it proceeds. Parlett and King (1971) discuss an innovation at MIT where switching from 'distributed' to 'concentrated' study led to reduction in lecturing, developments of new role relationships between faculty and students, and greater interaction between the students themselves. Since the total impact of the innovation was greater than originally foreseen, assessment of stated objectives would have given a too limited view of it. They therefore claim that the evaluator should concentrate on 'process' within the learning milieu, rather than on 'outcomes' derived from a specification of the instructional system, and point out that the method 'involves the investigator leaving his office and computer print-out to spend substantial periods in the field'.

Although their method – which employs some of the approaches used by anthropologists and psychiatrists – is interesting and new in this context, their suggestion that most existing evaluation is based on designs introduced by biologists seems not to be wholly correct. In fact, very few investigations into teaching and learning in higher education are carefully controlled since most teachers resist any interference with their normal methods of working (see Beard and Bligh 1971). For this reason they commonly already give considerable weight to opinions about an innovation. Designs used by biologists are intended for experiments having representative samples which enable the scientist to generalize his conclusions to a larger population. In educational investigations this is rarely attempted.

In surveying results of American studies of teaching behaviour and student achievement in which experimental designs are often more sophisticated than those employed in Britain, Rosenshine (1971) frequently points out difficulty in interpreting results : 'Items in the observation scales.... seem to be related to clarity, but it is impossible to determine whether these items were measuring the same thing as was measured under "clarity" in other studies'; 'the results of these 16 studies are difficult to summarize because of the variation in the designs'; 'two studies are insufficient for any generalization'. 'One would think that the frequency of teacher-student interactions would be a simple variable to code.... This reviewer once thought so' ....and so on. In addition, since each experiment takes place with different students and teachers, in different colleges or schools, conditions vary almost unpredictably. Nevertheless, it is from a diversity of similar, small experiments, often rather poorly designed, that useful generalizations can at length be made. For instance, it is now possible to conclude that under certain circumstances, programmed learning may save considerable time, and that knowledge of results, especially if students discover their own errors, leads to more effective learning.

In addition, measurement techniques enable teachers and research workers to discover what the students have, in fact, learned and not what they or their teachers think they have learned. Some research workers have noted negligible correlations between students' ratings of courses and their performance in subsequent tests (Joyce and Weatherall 1957, Remmers et al. 1949, Russell and Bendig 1953) and, although this does not necessarily prove their opinions invalid, it does suggest that caution should be exercised in accepting them at face value.

Further, if, as Parlett and Hamilton suggest, the methods of biologists are sometimes used by research workers in education in such a way that results are out of date before they are obtained, or if many relevant factors are ignored, or the methods oblige students to work under abnormal conditions, this is less a criticism of the methods as such, than of the experimenters' understanding and use of them. The methods still have a place in answering well framed questions, some of which relate to the achievement of objectives, or in making predictions as to the success of methods in similar circumstances elsewhere. The careful, observational methods so strongly recommended by Parlett and his collaborators may be seen not as a replacement for traditional methods but as a valuable supplement to them.

CONCLUSIONS

In concluding this survey of evaluation techniques, we must stress that those discussed here are not adequately related to the objectives which we considered in Chapters 1 and 3. This will inevitably be the case until objectives have been defined in detail and with sufficient clarity to provide a basis for comprehensive evaluation of learning and teaching. There is no doubt that interest already exists in the university schools, but the volume of work involved in undertaking a detailed, and perhaps controversial, examination of objectives is formidable, nor can it be undertaken by an outsider. It must involve the teaching staff; for, however helpful a psychologist may be, he is unable to specify the objectives of other teachers in an unfamiliar field and, in any case, for the objectives to be fully meaningful to the teachers they must share in defining them.

Already there is an appreciation that in practising skills, or in learning information and principles, prompt feedback is desirable and that it should indicate not only what errors to avoid, but how to improve performance still further. There are a number of experiments in progress which are beginning to reach the point where departments can combine in preparing tests, in using and writing programmed books or sharing experiences of introducing open-ended experiments and research projects. As co-operation of this kind increases, ability to assist and to evaluate different kinds of learning will accelerate. In addition, it may lead to the development of new ways to evaluate learning as fresh objectives are identified and defined.

From the preceding discussion, it is also evident that there is much research to do. There are many skills and abilities which we neither teach nor evaluate adequately. We need to investigate their nature more fully and to devise techniques to evaluate successive steps in realizing them. It is pleasant to imagine a research centre which could undertake this for all university schools and certainly more research staff would be valuable, but we have already observed that, in higher education, psychologists may not fully understand the objectives of the teachers since the subject matter in other fields is too unfamiliar. In addition, there is a great deal to be said in favour of the teachers themselves (or at least a proportion of them) being involved in developing new teaching methods and techniques of evaluation; for, in this way, they apply them with full understanding which can readily be shared with colleagues and, in seeing the resulting improvements in learning and teaching, all become more enthusiastic. Thus it seems probable that co-operation between teachers and relatively few psychologists and professional educationalists within the institution will be the most effective aid to progress.

APPENDIX A SOME EXAMPLES OF GENERAL OBJECTIVES

1 Examples of objectives for the development of skills in an undergraduate physics course (from Pole 1973)

(Where the skills concerned are required for effective study, they are commonly termed enabling objectives.)

II SKILLS

Objectives	Activities	Evaluation
II.1 Collection of information	II.1	II.1
II.1.1 Knowing where to find relevant information	Lecture from librarian on use of library, abstracts, bibliographies	Indirect evidence from essays and examination answers
II.1.2 Skimming through the literature to find specified information	Essays requiring information beyond that given in lectures	Assessment of essays with aid of checklist
II.1.3 Identifying important points and extracting the evidence from them	Students précis difficult material	Assessment of précis
	Preparation for project	Supervisor's impressions during discussion on project
II.1.4 Finding structure in difficult material	Sources of information given in reading lists etc.	Assessment of project
II.2 Application of the principles of physics	II.2	II.2
II.2.1 Using a given principle to solve a problem	Examples worked in lectures, demonstrations etc.	Assessment of practical work laboratory reports, etc.
II.2.2 Finding an appropriate principle to solve a given problem	Traditional practical work (set experiments with notes)	Specific examination questions (i) giving the principle to be applied (ii) not giving the principle
II.2.3 Idealizing a complex physical problem to one capable of solution by known principles	Students' private work (i) on book examples (ii) on previous examination papers	Assessment of projects, plus discussion with student
	Experimental and theoretical projects	

Objectives	Activities	Evaluation
II.3 Application of mathematical techniques	II.3 Continuous exposure to use of maths in all aspects of physics	II.3 Responses and suggestions in tutorials, classes etc.
II.3.1 Using a given technique in a given situation	Theoretical projects	Performance in projects
II.3.2 Selecting an appropriate technique in a given situation	Problem sheets and classes (i) where technique given (ii) where technique not given	Specific examination questions eg. 'What method would you use to solve the following problem...?'
II.3.3 Fitting a technique to a problem, adjusting both if necessary	II.3.3 Students analyse data obtained in laboratory	
II.3.4 Using a computer	II.3.4 Students write and run programme, tracing and eliminating errors	Success of programme
II.4 Application of experimental techniques	II.4	II.4
II.4.1 Using a given technique in a given situation	II.4.1 First-year practical work of a traditional kind	II.4.1 Traditional practical examinations
II.4.2 Selecting an appropriate technique in a given situation	II.4.2 and II.4.3 Second and third-year practical work (more open-ended)	II.4.2 and II.4.3 Discussion with and observation of student in laboratory
II.4.3 Adapting the technique to the problem	Project	Specific examination questions eg. 'What method would you use to...?'

Objectives	Activities	Evaluation
II.4.4 Extracting maximum information from a given situation	II.4.4 Experimental reports, noting alternative method(s) used, causes of failure etc. Students make proposals for further work	II.4.4 Assessment of reports, proposals, etc. Retrieval of information after a lapse of time
II.4.5 Estimating the limits of uncertainty	II.4.5 Lecture(s) on experimental errors and statistical techniques Discussion of experimental errors in students' practical reports Exercises with simulated data or with own data	II.4.5 Examination questions requiring analysis of experimental data
II.4.6 Designing experiments, taking account of practical and economic constraints	II.4.6 Third-year project work in consultation with demonstrators Hypothetical design exercises in tutorials	II.4.6 Assessment of project and report, noting quality of design
II.5 Flexibility in solving problems II.5.1 Recognizing and solving unfamiliar problems II.5.2 Realizing that there may be different ways of solving the same problem	II.5 Open-ended experiments, projects Alternative proofs given in lectures Attention drawn to analogies from other fields	II.5 Assessment of open-ended experiments and projects Specific examination questions eg. 'Solve the following problem by any method other than x....'

Objectives	Activities	Evaluation
II. 5. 3 Recognizing the similarity in solving problems in different areas of physics	Difficult and unorthodox problems set Use of analogue computer in laboratory Discussion of difficulties with tutor or demonstrator	Effective resolution of difficulties
II. 6 Evaluation in solving problems	II. 6 Presentation of information on scientific methods as part of practical course	II. 6
II. 6. 1 Recognizing when an adequate result has been obtained, in terms of time available, levels of accuracy etc. II. 6. 2 Assessing the accuracy of one's own work	II. 6. 1 and II. 6. 2 Discussion of experiments (i) by student in report (ii) with student during class	II. 6. 1 and II. 6. 2 Assessment of laboratory performance, reports, dissertations etc.
II. 6. 3 Finding mistakes and correction them	II. 6. 3 Check procedures described and practice in them provided 'Deliberate mistake' problems set	II. 6. 3 Time taken by student to spot errors Reassessment of corrected work

Objectives	Activities	Evaluation
II.6.4 Assessing the reliability of other's work	II.6.4 Discussion in class of other students' experimental work Students read journal articles that criticize other people's research	II.6.4 Standard of discussion
II.7 Interpretation and explanation	II.7 Project work, open-ended experiments	II.7 Assessment of project reports, laboratory notes, essays
II.7.1 Interpreting experimental observations	II.7.1 Experimental projects, involving data collection and analysis	
II.7.2 Drawing inferences from experimental results	II.7.2 Relation of two or more facts (or sets of data) from which conclusion is drawn	II.7.2 Validity of conclusions and supporting argument

2 Examples of objectives for a course for trainers of general practitioners
(prepared by R. Cox, N. Rea and D. Bennett in the University Teaching Methods Unit, University of London Institute of Education)

3.0 ASPECT

Teaching and management of learning

This aspect concerns the 'how' of teaching and learning with emphasis on the quality of the trainer/trainee interaction, becoming a more skilful practitioner in teaching and a more effective manager of learning. Management of learning will involve the organization of the practice and the local resources for learning but these are treated separately in Aspect 4.

The lack of any specification of the scope of knowledge expected of course members is particularly apparent here with the long list of topics in 11 to 13. This section functions here simply as a checklist for further detailed course planning. Other sections go into more detail and are more closely related to the specifications needed for particular aspects of the course.

3.1 ASSUMPTIONS

See Aspects 1 and 2

1 Tendency for many (but not all) members to leave trainees to pick up what they can from occasional discussions

2 Tendency to tell them the right answers

3 Little knowledge of education and educational psychology

3.2 VALUES AND GENERAL ORIENTATION OF THE COURSE

1 An active and directive policy of encouraging the trainee to ask the right questions, explore his own and others' assumptions and needs, to test their adequacy and come to his own conclusions within a comprehensive framework of the GP's role

2 Stress on importance of feedback for both trainer and trainee

3 Fostering independence so that the trainee will continue his education when the trainee year is over

3.3 Aims and objectives	3.4 Activities	3.5 What is to be assessed	3.6 Methods of assessment
Attitudes	Attitudes	Attitudes	Attitudes
Away from:			
1 Authoritarian and rigid attitudes	General activities for attitudes, knowledge and skills :	How far the course has influenced attitude objectives	Attitude questionnaires
2 Belief in the adequacy of a small range of teaching techniques	Reading		Interviews
	Lectures from course staff and visitors		Observation
3 Stereotyped view of trainee's motivation, expectations, style of working and interests	Group discussion and reporting		Written comment on teaching
	Demonstrations		
4 Regarding trainee as having a passive role	Role Play		
	Films, tapes, etc.		
	Projects		
	Syndicates		
	Particular activities related to attitudes (in addition to general activities)		

3.3 Aims and objectives	3.4 Activities	3.5 What is to be assessed	3.6 Methods of assessment
Towards : 5 Non-authoritarian flexible attitudes 6 Wanting to learn, apply and develop a wide range of techniques 7 Valuing independent activity of trainees and involvement of them in planning trainee year 8 Wanting to create a positive open, trusting, free and self-critical teaching and learning atmosphere 9 Wanting insight into trainee's expectations, motivation and performance 10 Wanting insight into own motivation and performance	Group discussion and role play with trainees		

Knowledge	Knowledge	Knowledge	Knowledge
11 Knowledge of principles of learning – communication problems - emotional aspects -feedback, motivation, reward and punishment -active and passive learning etc.	See general activities above	Not assessed directly See column 6	Expressed in attitudes and skills and in course members' statements and questions, discussions, interviews, reports and general feedback activities during the course
12 Knowledge of teaching/learning techniques lecturing use of aids tutorial - teaching/demonstrating on specific cases a medical aspects b interviewing aspects - small group discussion - case studies and reports - syndicate work - projects			

3.3 Aims and objectives	3.4 Activities	3.5 What is to be assessed	3.6 Methods of assessment
13 Knowledge of evaluation methods - observation techniques - interviewing - reports and questionnaires			
Skills	Skills	Skills	Skills
14 Ability to use variety of techniques (mentioned in K12 above) effectively in relation to different objectives	See general activities above and particular activities below. Preparation, delivery and criticism of short talks and case studies	Ability to prepare and deliver a lecture using appropriate aids. Ability to teach from consultations both in terms of :	See above (early and late in the course) Comparison of trainers' comments and criticisms of recorded teaching :
		a medical knowledge b interviewing consultation techniques	lectures role play group leadership
15 Ability to cope effectively with a wide range of teaching problems associated with different types of illness and different types of patients, including both sensitivity of trainee to doctor/patient relationships and medical treatment	Role play (of consultation and tutorials) acting observation and discussion Group discussion, acting as group leader Observation of groups Syndicate work reporting Project work reporting	Ability to prepare and give tutorials Ability to run and participate in group sessions Ability to guide project work	Evaluation of group self-criticism and analysis No direct evaluation possible with own trainee, except through interview Indications from attitude and teaching skill evaluations and from interviews

16 Ability to interact and develop an understanding relationship with the trainee which will make the teaching/learning process most effective	Role play, group discussions	Quality of interaction with trainee	Questionnaire Observation of role play and discussion Course members' ratings of role play behaviour
17 Ability to develop and use insight into own motivations and performance to improve teaching	Group discussion, motivation and self-knowledge	Level of insight into own behaviour and application to teaching	Evaluation of group reports on trainee programme Evaluation of group discussion on 'fit' and individual reports for specific trainees
18 Ability to fit general programme to individual needs	Group development of trainee programme Group discussion of problems of 'fit'	Ability to plan general programme for trainees Ability to fit general programme to individual needs	Assessment of group evaluation design reports Assessment of course members' evaluation of role play etc.
19 Ability to <u>select</u> appropriate techniques for particular objectives	Trainers and trainees devising individual programmes as group exercises		Assessment of course members evaluation of trainers course
20 Ability to organize objectives and methods into a meaningful programme for the trainee year with options to take account of individual differences	Case studies of programmes presented by trainers who have trainees		

3.3 Aims and objectives	3.4 Activities	3.5 What is to be assessed	3.6 Methods of assessment
21 Ability to liaise with colleagues in medical and non-medical areas, to arrange suitable exchanges, placements, follow-up of patients etc.	Interdisciplinary group discussions	Ability to liaise with colleagues	Observation of group discussions as examples of liaison and discussion of liaison issue
22 Ability to design and use a variety of assessment methods to analyse and improve both teaching and learning	Group development of assessment design Practice in evaluating role play, group work, reports and the trainers' course itself	Ability to design and use a variety of assessment methods : observation techniques interviewing (viva) reports	
23 Ability to integrate assessment methods into comprehensive meaningful design	Practice in assessment Interviewing	Questionnaires Ability to integrate different methods	

3 Examples of general objectives in the teaching of educational psychology

From: Stones, E. and Anderson, D. (1970)

AREA 2

The psychology of teaching cognitive skills

Level 1 objectives

Type A

given a teaching objective involving cognitive learning, decide on the type(s) of pupil learning most appropriate to the objective and specify the teaching and learning activities most likely to optimize the pupils' learning.

Type B

classify novel examples of teaching behaviour according to their appropriateness for different types of cognitive learning. (Given specimens of teaching behaviour, a student should be able to decide what kind of learning they are intended to produce.)

Type C

recall the key principles in teaching for efficient cognitive learning.

Notes

These objectives are closely related to areas 1 and 3 which deal with human learning and the teaching of motor skills respectively. They are dealt with separately as an aid to clarifying the concepts involved. A general point of some importance is that the objectives in this area are concerned with the way in which the teacher actively intervenes in the children's learning, whereas area 1 is concerned with a 'non interventional' approach to learning as an object of study. The type A objective involves highly complex activity on the part of the student, mainly at levels 5 and 6 of the Bloom taxonomy and at a high level of problem solving. This objective is an important link between psychological theory and the practice of teaching.

Type B objectives

Level 1: classify novel examples of teaching behaviour according to their appropriateness to the different types of cognitive learning. (Given specimens of teaching behaviour, a student should be able to decide what kind of pupil learning they are intended to produce.)

Which yields the following Level 2 objectives

1 distinguish between teaching situations which are likely to produce adaptive behaviour in pupils and those which are not;

2 distinguish between the different elements of entry behaviour in specific teaching/learning situations;

3 identify the elements in specific teaching/learning situations which exemplify the principles of cybernetics;

4 distinguish between exemplars and non-exemplars of teaching behaviour designed to produce classical conditioning;

5 distinguish between exemplars and non-exemplars of teaching behaviour designed to produce instrumental conditioning;

6 distinguish between exemplars and non-exemplars of teaching behaviour designed to produce response chaining;

7 distinguish between exemplars and non-exemplars of teaching behaviour designed to produce learning set formation;

8 distinguish between exemplars and non-exemplars of teaching behaviour designed to produce concept learning;

9 distinguish between exemplars and non-exemplars of teaching behaviour designed to produce principle learning;

10 distinguish between exemplars and non-exemplars of teaching behaviour designed to foster problem solving;

11 distinguish between specific examples of teaching behaviour appropriate to rote learning and that appropriate to meaningful learning.

* * * * *

Further examples of general objectives may be obtained from :

Beard (1972) Ch. II Industrial design, French language, French literature, history, physics

Dallas and Piper (1973) Training of biology teachers

Dressel et al. (1961) pp. 161-164, critical judgment in humanities

Dressel and Mayhew (1956) Humanities, including the pages mentioned above

APPENDIX B SOME EXAMPLES OF SPECIFIC OBJECTIVES

1 Examples of objectives for a mechanical engineering course (given by B.J. Hill at the conference on Objectives in Higher Education, held at the University of London Institute of Education 1969)

STATEMENT OF OBJECTIVES FOR A PROPOSED COURSE IN TURBULENT BOUNDARY LAYERS

(Department of Mechanical Engineering Imperial College)

Knowledge

a Students will be able to recall from memory :

1 the circumstances and qualitative features of the main tbl phenomena of thermal power and process engineering (flows in pipes and annuli; flow around aerofoils; film-cooling flows; free turbulent mixing layers, jets and wakes)

2 The distinction between a tbl and a turbulent separated flow, and the circumstances giving rise to each

3 the distinction between a two-dimensional and a three dimensional tbl and the circumstances giving rise to each

4 the qualitative features of the velocity, temperature, concentration and shear stress fields of tbl's and of their response to changes of Reynolds number, pressure gradient, mass transfer through a wall, and non-uniformity of fluid properties

5 the qualitative features of the phenomena of 'transition' and 'laminarization' and the circumstances giving rise to them

6 the nature, origin and limitations of the main hypotheses for the effective viscosity in a tbl, and of the implied effects of geometry, velocity profile, density variation, local Reynolds number

7 the partial differential equations of the two-dimensional tbl in Cartesian co-ordinates, and the integral momentum equation

b Students will be able to recognize and distinguish :

1 the partial differential equations of the 2D tbl in the following co-ordinate systems : Cartesian, von Miscs, general orthogonal

2 the following integral equations : momentum, mean motion, kinetic energy, moment of momentum, ϕ, ϕ^2, mass conservation, all for the 2D tbl

3 the ordinary differential equations of the Couette flow near a smooth wall with presence of mass transfer and pressure gradient, together with the main effective-transport-coefficient assumptions and the solution of the equations which are appropriate to them, expressed as laws of friction and heat transfer

4 the ordinary differential equations of the equilibrium 2D tbl together with the conditions giving rise to them and the qualitative features of their solutions

5 various versions of the functions **E** and **P** which express the influence of roughness, Prandtl/Schmidt number and mass transfer

6 the drag laws of Prandtl, Squire-Young, Schultz-Grunow and Escudier-Nicoll-Spalding for uniform-property 2D tbl's

7 the formulae of Eckert, Kutalteladze-Leont'ev and Spalding-Chi for the influence of Mach number and temperature ratio on drag

8 the superposition formulae allowing the calculation of the heat transfer from a surface of non-uniform temperature under circumstances of linearity

9 various of the $H_3 \sim H$ relations and the $s \sim H \sim R_2$ relations of the 2D tbl

Skill

a Students will be able to use :

1 the standard formulae for pressure drop and heat transfer in round smooth-walled pipes, with account for effects of non-uniform properties

2 the formulae for the skin friction and heat transfer of smooth flat plates, with account for influences of mass transfer and of non-uniform properties

3 the explicit method of predicting the uniform property hydrodynamic boundary layer, based on the momentum and mean-kinetic-energy equations

4 the Ambrok method of predicting heat transfer, with account for non-uniform wall temperature

5 the momentum equation for two halves of a free turbulent boundary layer for predicting the rate of spread of a plane mixing layer jet or wake

6 empirical algebraic formulae for the prediction of the effectiveness of a film-cooling system in the absence of a longitudinal pressure gradient

7 experimental data on an inert-fluid free-turbulent flow for the prediction of flame length in similar circumstances

b Students will be able to derive :

1 velocity and temperature profiles in Couette flows from prescribed transport-property assumptions, when the density is uniform

2 pressure drop and heat-transfer relations for flow in smooth pipes, from the profile formulae of Couette flows

3 the solution for the velocity profile in a plane mixing layer between streams of nearly equal velocity, from the partial differential equation and the Prandtl-Tollmien mixing length assumptions

5 the KE -of-mean-motion equation from the partial differential equation for plane uniform-property flow

6 the conditions for the existence of equilibrium boundary layers

c Students will be able to determine :

1 the basic assumptions and the computational procedure of methods of tbl prediction which they encounter in the literature

2 the best method of prediction to use for common circumstances arising in engineering practice

* * * *

SPECIMEN SYLLABUS STATEMENTS FOR THE POSTGRADUATE COURSE THERMAL POWER AND PROCESS ENGINEERING

(Department of Mechanical Engineering Imperial College)

1 Numerical Analysis (TPP. 21)

About 10 lectures in the spring term.

Aim of course

To inform students on mathematical formulation of various problems in engineering and science

To teach students to analyse these problems

To teach students to use finite-difference techniques to obtain numerical results

Syllabus

a Knowledge

Students will be able to recognize and distinguish :

i Partial differential equations in two and three variables and in Cartesian and polar co-ordinate systems

ii Second order differential equations of elliptical, parabolic and hyperbolic type

iii Finite-difference formulation of partial differential equations

iv Rectangular, polar or irregular network for finite-difference together with judicious choice for each problem

v Boundary conditions and their role in solving the problem

vi Linear algebraic equations and methods of solving, using : elimination, iteration or relaxation

vii Explicit and implicit methods and their advantages and disadvantages

viii Discretization and truncation error and a way of improving the accuracy of the solutions

ix Convergence and stability of finite difference equations

b Skills

Students will be able to :

i Analyse various problems in heat transfer, fluid mechanics and applied mechanics

ii Perform a technique to solve partial differential equations even with complicated boundary conditions

iii Select the best network for finite difference, ie. rectangular, polar or irregular, depending on the shape of the domain

iv Select the best method for solving a set (or several sets) of linear algebraic equations

v Make judicious choice of the spacing of the finite-difference network in order to obtain sufficient accuracy depending on the nature of each particular problem

2 Equipment design (TPP. 17)

About 10 lectures in the spring term

Aim of course

To make students aware of the nature of thermal design; the influence of considerations of cost; and the variety and sources of analytical and empirical design data

To teach students procedures and techniques of thermal design

Syllabus

Students will not be required to perform mechanical design or drawing-board work. There will however be course-work in the form of tutorial exercises, one of which will require the writing of a computer programme. Most of the illustrations and exercises used in the course will relate to stationary thermal equipment such as heat exchangers, cooling towers, steam condensers and their component parts and processes.

It is intended that students who attend the course will attain the following level of performance :

a Knowledge and comprehension

i the aims of engineering design; the variety of activities that may be necessary for the achievement of these aims; the scope of thermal design

ii the need for and the nature of a thermal design specification and the complete design specification of which it is a part

iii the kinds and sources of data used in thermal design

iv the contribution to design of mathematical models and analogies and optimization procedures

b Skills

The student will be able to :

i recognize the status (dependent or independent) of the variables in a design problem

ii extract from scattered experimental data empirical rules and coefficients for use in design

iii deduce formulae for optimum values of parameters in particular cases iv specify the additional data necessary for preparing a design for a particular thermal specification

v compare the relative merit of different forms of equipment which satisfy a particular technical specification by reference to economic considerations

vi prepare a computer programme for calculating the principal parameters of a range of designs for a particular thermal specification and the optimum values of these parameters

3 Experimental Methods (TPP.18)

About 10 lectures in the autumn term

Aim of course

The course is intended to :

i focus students' attention on, and enhance their knowledge of, methods of instrumentation and experimental techniques commonly employed in fluid dynamics, combustion, heat and mass transfer

ii equip students with the background knowledge needed to guide them in the selection and use of instrumentation employed in thermo-dynamics sciences

iii provide concise logical explanations of the theory and function of the apparatus and techniques described in the course which draw upon, connect with and extend students' analytical knowledge and training

iv provide sufficient openings by means of references to the literature etc., to enable students to pursue any aspect of the subject matter to greater depth than is possible in the course of lectures

students successfully completing the course will be expected to acquire the following knowledge and skills

Syllabus

a Knowledge

A general knowledge of the following techniques and the principal sources of error to which they are subject :

i Temperature measurements with solid bodies, on the surface of solids and in fluid streams by means of thermocouples, resistance methods, fusible plugs, thermal radiation instruments, pneumatic probes, intermittent pyrometers ii Pressure measurements in flowing streams by means of pitot and pitot-static probes, also the use of Preston and Stanton tubes in boundary layer work. Capacitive, inductive, piezoelectric and resistance strain-gauge type pressure transducers

iv Mass flow measurements by means of orifice, nozzle and ventural meters, pitot traverse technique, rotameters, positive displacement and electro-magnetic flow meters, laminar flow meters, calorimetric meters

v Measurements of concentration in binary mixtures by acoustic, visco-metric and thermal conductivity techniques also concentration measurements in gaseous mixtures of more than two constituents by infra-red gas analysis, chromatography and mass spectrometry

vi Flow visualization by means of tufts, tracers, ointments, Schlieren, shadow and interferometric methods

vii Measurement of heat flux by radial flow transducers, thermal resistance sandwich, calorimetric and transient techniques

viii Measurement of calorific value by means of constant pressure gas and bomb type calorimeters

ix Viscosity measurements in Newtonian and non-Newtonian fluids by means of a capillary, efflux, falling sphere, rotating element and oscillatory viscometers

x Measurement of thermal conductivities in gases, liquids and solids, and measurement of diffusion coefficients by the Loschmidt column, Stefan and point source methods

xi Recording techniques and inclined tube, averaging and precision type manometers, pressure gauges, temperature recorders, chart recorders, oscilloscopes and photographic equipment

b <u>Skills</u>

Students will be expected to be able to :

i identify the merits and disadvantages of the particular techniques covered in the course, and recognize sources of error in the results obtained with them

ii exhibit an understanding of the principles of the apparatus and techniques described in the course

iii choose types of instrumentation suitable for specified duties iv Design, or compile the specifications for, instrumentation commonly used in fluid dynamics, combustion, heat and mass transfer experimentation

v Identify, and recognize the limitations of, techniques suitable for the measurement of unsteady phenomena

vi Demonstrate familiarity with commonly used types of temperature and pressure measuring equipment

vii Identify and use the Rayleigh pitot formula

viii Derive relationships for dynamic head in terms of pressure and temperature

ix Derive expressions for the mass flow through meters of the orifice, nozzle venturi and viscous flow types

x Derive differential equations defining the flow of heat along the leads and supports of thermocouples

xi Derive the transient heat conduction equation and establish the Binder-Schmidt solution in its one-dimensional form

xii Show that an interferometer may be used as a means of measuring the density of a flowing, compressible, fluid, and derive relationships which demonstrate that the local intensity of illumination of images produced by Schlieren and shadow methods of flow visualization is proportional to the first and second derivatives of density gradient respectively.

2 Examples of learning objectives from the beginning of a chapter in Davis (1971):

LEARNING OBJECTIVES

Cognitive objectives

After carefully reading this chapter, you will be able to :

1 distinguish between an aim and an objective

2 state four reasons for specifying objectives

3 recognize and discriminate between cognitive, affective and psychomotor objectives

4 list four ways in which Bloom's taxonomy can be useful to the teacher or instructor

5 state what words should be avoided and what words should be used when writing clear objectives

6 list, and write short notes upon, the three types of information essential to a clear objective

7 write a clear objective using either the Mager or the Miller system

Affective objectives

After reading this chapter, the author intends that you will :

1 be aware of, and value, the importance of clear objectives to the learning process

2 incorporate into your teaching behaviour either the Miller of Mager system of writing objectives

* * * *

Further examples of specific objectives may be obtained from :

Bloom, Hastings and Madeus (1971) A diversity of subjects, mainly at school level

C. Engel has a collection of objectives in medical education at the Department of Audio-Visual Communication, BMA, Tavistock Square, London

Kibler, Harker and Miles (1970) A diversity of subjects, mainly at school level

3 Example of objectives from an appendix in Ross, D. (1974) (Ross, with colleagues, worked out a course under four headings: Objective, Planned student experience/activity, Materials/equipment to be prepared/available, Method of evaluation.) The part of the course from day 51 to day 64 dealing with Civil Litigation appears as an appendix to a discussion of the course and methods.

DAY 52 — CIVIL LITIGATION (contd.)

Objective	Planned student experience/activity	Materials/equipment to be prepared/available	Method of evaluation
7 to recall in relation to pre-litigation correspondence (a) what constitutes a 'without prejudice' letter, and what is the effect of such a letter (b) the dangers of extensive pre-trial correspondence (c) the possible need for pre-trial action (i) to rescind a contract or give appropriate notice (ii) to make a formal demand (iii) to tender (iv) self-serving correspondence (d) that no party and party costs are allowed except for a letter of demand	7 -Lecture/discussion by instructor on pre-litigation correspondence and pre-trial action in general -Reinforcement in 8	7 Lecture outline to be prepared in advance for handing to each student before the lecture begins	7 -Instructors to note informally whether students demonstrate their grasp of the content of the lecture by answers to questions or other participation -Indirectly tested by evaluation of 8
8 to decide the appropriate pre-trial action in given cases and to be able to (a) draft (i) pre-litigation correspondence (ii) a letter of demand (b) tender (c) send notices (i) to the Incorporated Nominal Defendant (ii) of recission under a contract of sale of land (iii) in a detinue claim (iv) calling up a mortgage	8 -Students to be required to draft tender and send notices in response to prepared problems. This will be a long exercise -Reinforcement of Commercial Law Practice Objectives 15 & 16, and conveyancing objective 3 (b) -Reinforcement by later provision of model correspondence and notices and by discussion presided over by instructors to examine the questions and answers in detail	8 -Numerous fact situations to be prepared requiring action appropriate to this objective: these will need engrossing substantially in advance if it is intended that they be duplicated for distribution to each student -Model correspondence and notices to be prepared in advance for handing to each student at the completion of this exercise	8 -Instructors to supervise the work of students and to be on hand to assess and, if necessary, correct student work

9 (a) to recall the jurisdictional characteristics of the Magistrates' Court, the County Court and the Supreme Court by reason of (i) the amount involved (ii) the relief sought (iii) the cause of action (b) to recognize the available jurisdictions in given cases and select the one appropriate	9 -All students to participate in group discussion conducted by an appointed student, for the purpose of compiling a comparative chart of jurisdictions (for the function of such a group see Instructors Guide Part 2) -At the completion of the group discussion, each student to be handed the prepared chart. Reinforcement by informal discussion led by instructors on the accuracy and use of such charts	9 -Comparative chart of jurisdictions to be prepared in advance for handing to each student at the completion of this activity -The following materials are to be available for the student group discussion: Justices Act County Court Act (S. 37) Supreme Court Act (S. 15-19) Instruments Act	9 Informal evaluation by instructors
<u>PART B</u> to conduct a simple case using the Magistrates' Court as an example	<u>PART B</u>	<u>PART B</u> The following fact situation to be prepared for the implementation of this part. The complainant is a tradesman seeking to recover the price of his labour and materials. The Defendant tenders a lesser amount representing what he says is a fair and reasonable price	<u>PART B</u>
10 In the given case in the Magistrates' Court, to (a) prepare the appropriate summons (b) draw the Particulars of Demand (c) select the venue, and the return date (d) locate the fee payable on issue (e) issue the summons	10 -Students to be shown a sample summons and Particulars of Demand -Thereafter each student to carry out what this objective requires -Reinforcement by later provision of model document. Also informal discussion led by instructors upon the correctness of the model -Reinforcement in 25 and 42	10 -Sample summons to be prepared (involving a cause of action different from Part B) for demonstration purposes -each student to be handed the complainant's instructions -Model summons and particulars of demand to be prepared for handing to each student at the completion of the exercise	10 -Instructors to supervise and if necessary correct student work -Indirectly assessed by evaluation of 25 and of 42

APPENDIX C AN ANALYSIS RELATING TYPES OF ASSESSMENT WITH OBJECTIVES

(Suggested by D.A. Bligh 1972 b)

TYPE OF ASSESSMENT	SOME POSSIBLE OBJECTIVES ASSESSED	SOME POSSIBLE ADVANTAGES	SOME POSSIBLE DISADVANTAGES
Three hour essay exam	Knowledge of information Verbal fluency	Seem to be easy to set	Unreliable marking Emphasis on writing speed Poor coverage of syllabus Poor feedback
Prepared essay exam	Skills in preparation eg. seeking information Thought	Higher standards set by students Closer to 'real life'	No valid method of marking yet designed
Open book essay exams One long essay exam	Reference techniques Thought Depth of thought	Less study time spent on memorizing Inter-disciplinary answers obtained	Atypical performance
Course work	Motivation	Closer to vocational situation	Anxiety throughout course
Short answer questions	Knowledge of information	Broader coverage of syllabus More reliable marking	Little opportunity to display argument of originality
Projects Dissertations Theses	Ability to seek information, to reason Presentation techniques Interest/motivation Originality		No objectivity in marking Grading almost meaningless
Multiple choice questions (of various kinds)	Information Thought of all kinds Attitudes	A wide range of objectives Broad coverage of syllabus Objective marking	Difficult to set
Practicals	Practical (motor) skills Experimental design and techniques Application of principles		Written report rather than practical skill is assessed Cheating
Simulated tasks	Personal interaction Application of knowledge	Closely approximates to professional work	Careful preparation of marker's checklist necessary
Oral situations eg. viva or group discussion	Personal interaction Reasoning behind personal thought	Flexible Useful to confirm other assessments	Very subjective 'Halo' effect Examiner's skill

REFERENCES AND BIBLIOGRAPHY

ABERCROMBIE, M.L.J. (1960) The anatomy of judgment, Hutchinson, London

ABERCROMBIE, M.L.J. (1966) Perception and communication, in Teaching methods in university departments of science and medicine, report of a conference held at the University of London Institute of Education, January 1966 (out of print)

ADAMS, B.G., DANIEL, E.E., HERXHEIMER, A. and WEATHERALL, M. (1960) The value of emphasis in eliminating errors. British Medical Journal, 1960 (2), 1007-1011

ASCH, S.E. (1940) Studies in the principles of judgments and attitudes II : determination of judgments by group and ego standards. Journal of Social Psychology, SPSSI Bulletin 12, 433-465

ASCH, S.E. (1948) The doctrine of suggestion, prestige and imitation in social psychology. Psychological Review, 55

ASCH, S.E. (1956) Studies of independence and conformity I : A minority of one against a common majority. Psychological Monographs, 70, 9, Whole No. 416

ASH, P. and CARLTON, B.J. (1953) The value of note-taking during film learning. British Journal of Educational Psychology, 23, 121-125

BARBER, T.X. and CALVERLEY, D.S. (1963) 'Hypnotic like' suggestibility in children and adults. Journal of Abnormal and Social Psychology, 66, 589-597

BARCLAY, T.B. (1957) Effective reading. University of Edinburgh Gazette, 17, 22-30

BARNETT, S.A. (1958) An experiment with free discussion groups. Universities Quarterly, 12, 175-180

BAUME, D. and JONES, B. (1972) Handbook on aims and objectives, N.E. London Polytechnic, unpublished

BEARD, R.M., LEVY, P.M. and MADDOX, H. (1964) Academic performance at university. Educational Review, 16, 3, 163-174

BEARD, R.M. (1967) An inquiry into small group discussion methods in three disciplines. University Teaching Methods Research Unit, University of London Institute of Education

BEARD, R.M. (1967 a) On evaluating the success of teaching. British Journal of Medical Education, 1 (4), 296-302

BEARD, R.M. (1969) A conspectus of research and development, in The assessment of undergraduate performance, report of the Universities Spring Conference, 1969, convened by the Committee of Vice-Chancellors and Principals and the Association of University Teachers, London, Committee of Vice-Chancellors and Principals

BEARD, R.M. (1971) Programmed learning – co-operative ventures. Chemistry in Britain, 7 (8), 324-326

BEARD, R.M. and BLIGH, D.A. (1971a) Research into teaching methods in higher education, 3rd edition, London, Society for Research into Higher Education

BEARD, R.M. and POLE, K.E. (1971) Content and purpose of biochemistry exams. British Journal of Medical Education, 5, 13-21

BEARD, R.M. (1972) Teaching and learning in higher education, 2nd edition, Harmondsworth, Penguin

BERG, H.D. in P.L. DRESSEL et al. (1961) Evaluation in higher education, Boston, Mass., Houghton Mifflin

BERLYNE, D.E. (1954) An experimental study of human curiosity. British Journal of Psychology, 45, 256-265

BERNSTEIN, B. (1971) On the classification and framing of educational knowledge, in M.F.D. Young (ed.), Knowledge and control, New York, Collier MacMillan

BIRAN, L.A. and PICKERING, E. (1968) Unscrambling a herringbone: an experimental evaluation of a branching programming. British Journal of Medical Education, 2, 213-219

BLAUG, M. (1968) Universities and productivity, paper presented at the Universities Conference, March 1968

BLAUG, M. and WOODHALL, M. (1965) Productivity trends in British university education, 1938-62. Minerva, September, 483-499

BLIGH, D.A. (1972) What's the use of lectures? Harmondsworth, Penguin

BLIGH, D.A. (1972 a) Educational technology – an approach to educational decisions. Overseas Universities, August

BLOOM, B.S. (ed.) (1954) Taxonomy of educational objectives. Handbook I: cognitive domain, New York, D. McKay and Co.

BLOOM, B.S. (ed.) (1956) Taxonomy of educational objectives. Handbook II: affective domain, New York, D. McKay and Co.

BLOOM, B.S., HASTINGS, J.T. and MADEUS, G.F. (1971) Handbook of formative and summative evaluation of student learning, New York, McGraw Hill

BRISTOW, T. (1970) A reading seminar. The Library College Journal, 3 (3), 13-22

BRITISH MEDICAL STUDENTS' ASSOCIATION (1965) Report on medical education: suggestions for the future, London, BMA

BROCKBANK, P. (1968) Examining exams. The Times Literary Supplement, No. 3465, 781-782

BULL, G.M. (1956) An examination of the final examination in medicine. Lancet, 25 August, 368-372

BURGE, R.E. (1968) Wider London B.Sc. Times Educational Supplement, 1 March

CARTER, C.F. (1968) The productivity of universities: an economist's view, paper presented at the Universities Conference, Spring 1968

CHOWDHRY, S.H. and VERNON, P.E. (1964) An experimental study of imagery and its relation to abilities and interests. British Journal of Psychology, 55 (3), 355-364

COLLIER, K.G. (1966) An experiment in university teaching. Universities Quarterly, 20 (3), 336-348

CONNOR, D.V. (1967) A study of problem solving in physics. Australian Journal of Higher Education, 3 (1), 55-67

COTTON, T. and PETERSEN, O.L. (1967) An essay of medical students' abilities by oral examination. Journal of Medical Education, 42, 1005-1014

COTTRELL, T.L. (1962) Effect of size of tutorial group on teaching efficiency. University of Edinburgh Gazette, 33, 20-21

CROSSLEY, C.A. (1968) Tuition in the use of the library and of subject literature in the University of Bradford. Journal of Documentation, 24, 91-97

CROXTON, P.C.L. and MARTIN, L.H. (1965) Away with notes (programming in higher education). New Education, 1 (14), 25-27

DE CECCO, P. (1964) Class size and co-ordinated instruction. British Journal of Educational Psychology, 34 (1), 65-74

DALE, R.R. (1959) University standards. Universities Quarterly, 13, 187-195

DALLAS, D. and PIPER, D.W. Studies in course design 2: training of biology teachers, in preparation, obtainable from University of London Institute of Education, University Teaching Methods Unit

DAVIES, I.K. (1971) The management of learning, Maidenhead, McGraw Hill

DRESSEL, P.L. and MAYHEW, L.B. (1956) Critical analysis and judgement in the humanities, Dubuque, Iowa, William Brown Company

DRESSEL, P.L. et al. (1961) Evaluation in higher education, Boston, Mass., Houghton Mifflin

DUCKWORTH, R. (1966) An evaluation of two methods of teaching the principles of pathology to dental students. British Dental Journal, 121 (5), 218-221

ELLEY, W.B. (1966) The role of errors in learning with feedback. British Journal of Educational Psychology, 31 (3), 296-300

ELTON, C.F. (1965) The effect of logic instruction on the Valentine Reasoning Test. British Journal of Educational Psychology, 35 (3), 339-341

ELTON, L.R.B. (1968) The assessment of students – a new approach. Universities Quarterly, 22 (3), 291-301

ELTON, L.R.B. (1968) Success and failure in university physics courses. Physics Education, 3, 323

ENGEL, C. and WAKEFORD, R. (1973) An introduction to learning objectives, Departmental reprint, London, Department of Audiovisual Communication, British Medical Association

ERAUT, M. (1970) Course development : an approach to the improvement of teaching in higher education. Journal of Educational Technology, 1 (3), 195-206

ERSKINE, C.A. and O'MORCHOE, C.C.C. (1961) Research on teaching methods : its significance for the curriculum. Lancet, 1961 (2), 709-711

ERSKINE, C.A. and TOMKIN, A. (1963) Evaluation of the effect of the group discussion method in a complex training programme. Journal of Medical Education, 38, 1036-1042

EVANS, L.R., INGERSOLL, R.W. and SMITH, E.J. (1966) The reliability, validity and taxonomic structure of the oral examination. Journal of Medical Education, 41, 651-657

FESTINGER, L. and MACCOBY, N. (1964) On resistance to persuasive communications. Journal of Abnormal and Social Psychology, 68 (4), 359-366

FREYBERG, P.S. (1965) The effectiveness of note-taking. Education for Teaching, February, 17-24

FURST, E.J. (1957) Constructing evaluation instruments, London, Longmans Green

GAGNÉ, R.M. (1965) The conditions of learning, New York, Holt, Rinehart and Winston

GARDINER, Q., BODDY, F.A. and TAYLOR, J. (1969) An orientation course for first year medical students. British Journal of Medical Education, 3 (3), 199-201

GAUVAIN, S. (1968) The use of student opinion in the quality control of teaching. British Journal of Medical Education, 2 (1), 55-62

GERARD, H.B. (1964) Conformity and commitment to the group. Journal of Abnormal and Social Psychology, 68 (2), 209-211

GLYNN, E. (1965) Keys to chemistry (a personal effort in programming). New Education, 1 (10), 21-22

GORDON, W.J.J. (1961) Synectics, the development of creative capacity, New York, Harper and Row

GRAVES, J. and GRAVES, V. (1965) Medical sound recording, London and New York, Focal Press

GRAVES, J. and GRAVES, V. (eds.) (1967) Papers from the second conference on the use of audiotape in medical teaching, Held at the Academic Unit, Chelmsford and Essex Hospital, Chelmsford, Essex

GUGEON, D. et al. (1972) Draft unit on course tuition, Open University, discussion document, privately circulated

HALLWORTH, H.J. (1957) Group discussion in its relevance to teaching training. Educational Review, 10, 41-53

HAMMOND, K.R. and KERN, F. (1959) Teaching comprehensive medical care : a psychological study of a change in medical education, Cambridge, Mass. Harvard University Press

HARTLEY, H.J. (1968) Programme budgeting and cost-effectiveness in local schools, Paris, OECD, April

HAYES, D.M. (1964) Objective evaluation of a subjective teaching method : the student dissertation. Journal of Medical Education, 39, 1083-1089

HILL, K.R. and SCHEUER, P. A rapid reading course. Royal Free Hospital Journal, 29, 23-25

HIRST, P. (1967) Liberal education and the nature of knowledge, in Archambault, R. (ed.) Philosophical analysis and education, London, Routledge and Kegan Paul

HOARE, D.E. and INGLIS, G.R. (1965) Programmed learning in chemistry II : an experiment. Education in Chemistry, 2 (1), 32-35

HOLLAND, W.W., GARRAD, J., BENNETT, A.E. and RHODES, P. (1966) A clinical approach to the teaching of social medicine : an evaluation of an experimental method. Lancet, 1966 (1), 540-542

HOLLOWAY, P.J. (1964) A test of the use of a teaching aid for the instruction of undergraduate dental students in operative techniques. The Dental Practitioner, 14, 375-377

HOLLOWAY, P.J. (1966) The effect of lecture time on learning. British Journal of Educational Psychology, 31 (3), 255-258

HUBBARD, J.P. and CLEMENS, W.V. (1961) Multiple-choice examinations in medicine : a guide for examiners and examinee, Philadelphia, Pa., Lea and Febiger

HUDSON, L. (1966) Contrary imaginations : a psychological study of the English schoolboy, London, Methuen

HULL, C.L. (1933) Hypnosis and suggestibility : an experimental approach, New York, Appleton Century

HUXLEY, T.H. (1905) Collected essays Vol. 3 : science and education, London, Macmillan

INHELDER, B. and PIAGET, J. (1959) The growth of logical thinking, London, Routledge and Kegan Paul

JACOB, P.E. (1957) Changing values in colleges, New York, Harper

JAHODA, M. and THOMAS, L. (1966) The mechanics of learning. New Scientist, 30, 114-117

JAMES, D.W., JOHNSON, M.L. and VENNING, P. (1956) Testing for learnt skill in observation and evaluation of evidence. Lancet, 1956 (2), 379-383

JASPERS, K. (1960) The idea of the university (ed. K.W. Deutsch), London, Owen

JEVONS, F.R. (1970) Liberal studies in science – a successful experiment. Education in Chemistry, 7 (3), 98-99

JONES, G. (1965) Organic research projects in an undergraduate course. Education in Chemistry, 2 (5), 230-240

JONES, R.T. (1969) Multiform assessment : a York experiment. Cambridge Review, 15, 43-47

JOYCE, C.R.B. and WEATHERALL, M. (1957) Controlled experiments in teaching. Lancet, 1957 (2), 402-407

JOYCE, C.R.B. and WEATHERALL, M. (1959) Effective use of teaching time. Lancet, 1959 (1), 568-571

JUDY, R.W., LEVINE, J.B., WILSON, R. and WALTER, J. (1968) Systems analysis of alternative designs of a faculty, Paris, OECD, 3-5 April

KATONA, G. (1940) Organizing and memorizing, New York, Columbia University Press

KELLEY, E.C. (1947) Education for what is real, New York, Harper

KERSCH, B.Y. (1962) The classroom simulator. Journal of Teacher Education, 13, 109-110

KIBLER, R.J., BARKER, L. and MILES, D.T. (1970) Behavioural objectives and instruction, Boston, Mass., Allyn and Bacon

KING, B.T. and IRVING, J.L. (1956) Comparison of the effectiveness of improvised versus non-improvised role-playing in producing opinion changes. Human Relations, 9, 177-186

KORST, D.R. (1973) A guide to the clinical clerkship in medicine, Madison, Wisconsin, University of Wisconsin Medical School

LEITH, G.O.M. and BUCKLE, G.F. (1966) Mode of response and non-specific background knowledge, National Centre for Research and Documentation of Programmed Learning, University of Birmingham

LEITH, G.O.M. and McHUGH, G.A.R. (1967) The place of theory in learning consecutive conceptual tasks. Educational Review, 19 (2), 110-117

LEWIN, K. (1947) Group decision and social change, in Newcomb, T.M. and Hartley, E.L. (eds.) Readings in social psychology, New York, Holt

LEWIS, B.N. (1971, 1972) Course production at the Open University (a) some basic problems; (b) activities and activity networks; (c) planning and scheduling. British Journal of Educational Technology, 2, 4-13, 111-123; 3, 189-204

LORGE, I. (1936) Prestige, suggestion and attitudes. Journal of Social Psychology, 7, 386-402

LYSAUGHT, J.P. and WILLIAMS, C.M. (1963) A guide to programmed instruction, New York, Wiley

MACLAINE, A.G. (1963) An experiment with closed circuit television at the University of Sydney. Australian Journal of Education, 7 (3), 157-164

McLEISH, J. (1966) Student retention of lecture material : a methodological study. Cambridge Institute of Education Bulletin, 3 (3), 2-11

McLEISH, J. (1968) The lecture method, Cambridge Monographs on Teaching Methods No. 1, Cambridge Institute of Education

McGUIRE, C. (1963) A process approach to the construction and analysis of medical examinations. Journal of Medical Education, 38 (7), 556

McKEACHIE, W.J. (1966) Research in teaching : the gap between theory and practice, in Improving college teaching, American Council on Education

MACKENZIE, N., ERAUT, M. and JONES, H.C. (1970) Teaching and learning : an introduction to new methods and resources in higher education, Paris, UNESCO

MAGER, R.F. (1962) Preparing instructional objectives, San Francisco, Calif., Fearon

MAIER, N.R.F. (1930) Reasoning in humans I: on direction. Journal of Comparative Psychology, 10, 115-143

MANN, P.H. and MILLS, G. (1961) A study of universities section III : living and learning at Redbrick : I academic conditions. Universities Quarterly, 16, 19-24

McFARLANE SMITH, I. (1973) A study of changes in attitude to teaching of students attending a college of education (technical). Higher Education 2, 361-373

McGUIRE, C. (1964) The process approach to the evaluation of medical curricula: theory and practice, paper presented at a conference on medical education in South Africa

MEALINGS, R.J. (1963) Problem solving in science teaching. Educational Review, 15, 194-207

MILLER, G. (ed.) (1962) Teaching and learning in medical school, Cambridge, Mass., Harvard University Press

MOORE, D. (1967) Group teaching by programmed instruction. Programmed Learning and Educational Technology, 4 (1), 37-46

MOORE, R.A. (1954) Methods of examining students in medicine. Journal of Medical Education, 29 (1), 23-27

MOSEL, J.N. (1964) The learning process. Journal of Medical Education, 39, 485-496

NAERAA, N. (1972) Objectives for a course in physiology for medical students, Aarhus, Denmark, University of Aarhus

NEDELSKY, L. (1949) Formulation of objectives of teaching in the physical sciences. American Journal of Physics, 17, 345-354

NEWMAN, J.H. (1949 reprint) On the scope and nature of university education, Everyman's Library edition

NEWMAN, J.H. (1929 edition) The idea of a university, London, Longmans Green

OAKESHOTT, M. (1962) Rationalization in politics and other essays, London, Methuen

ORTEGA Y GASSET, J. (1946) The mission of the university, Part of International Library of Sociology and Social Reconstruction, London, Routledge and Kegan Paul

OWEN, S.G., HALL, R., ANDERSON, J. and SMART, G.A. (1965) A comparison of programmed instruction and lectures in the teaching of electrocardiography. Programmed Learning, 2, 2-14

PALMER, O.E. (1961) Evaluation of communication skills, in P.L. Dressel et al. Evaluation in higher education, Boston, Mass., Houghton Mifflin

PARKHURST, H. (1930) Education on the Dalton Plan, London, Bell and Son

PARLETT, M. and KING, J.G. (1971) Concentrated study: a pedagogic innovation observed, London, Society for Research into Higher Education

PARLETT, M. and HAMILTON, D. (1972) Evaluation as illumination : a new approach to the study of innovatory programmes, occasional paper 9, Centre for Research in the Educational Sciences, University of Edinburgh

PEEL, E.A. (1966) A study of differences in the judgment of adolescent pupils. British Journal of Educational Psychology, 36, 77-86

PETERS, R.S. (1966) Ethics and education, London, Allen and Unwin

PETERSEN, A.D.C. (1960) Arts and science sides in the sixth form, London, Gulbenkian Foundation Report

PIPER, D.W. (1967) Strategies in course planning. Design Education 2, 16-18 London, Hornsey College of Art

POLE, K. (1973) Studies in course design I : physics, in preparation, obtainable from University of London Institute of Education, University Teaching Methods Unit

POPHAM, J.W. (1972) An evaluation guidebook, Los Angeles, California, The Instructional Objectives Exchange

POPPLETON, P.K. and AUSTWICK, K. (1964) A comparison of programmed learning and note-taking at two age levels. British Journal of Educational Psychology, 34 (1), 43-50

POULTON, E.C. (1961) British courses for adults on effective reading. British Journal of Educational Psychology, 31, Part II, 128-137

PRING, R. (1971) Bloom's taxonomy : a philosophical critique 2. Cambridge Journal of Education, 2, 83-91

REMMERS, H.H., MARTIN, S.D. and ELLIOTT, D.N. (1949) Are students' ratings of instructors related to their grades? Purdue University Studies in Higher Education, 66, 17-26

ROMISZOWSKI, A.J. (1967) A survey of the use of programmed learning in industry during 1966. Programmed Learning and Educational Technology, 4 (3), 210-215

ROSENSHINE, B. (1971) Teaching behaviours and student achievement, Slough, National Foundation for Educational Research

ROSS, D. (1974) A postgraduate skills course as a pre-requisite to legal practice in Victoria — devising a blueprint for design, implementation and evaluation, Leo Cussen Institute for Continuing Legal Education, 497 La Trobe Street, Melbourne, Victoria 3000

ROWNTREE, D. (1970) Learn how to study, London, Macdonald

RUSSELL, H.E. and BENDIG, A.W. (1953) Investigation of the relations of student ratings of psychology instructors to their course achievement when academic aptitude is controlled. Educational and Psychological Measurement, 13, 626-635

SCHOOLS COUNCIL FOR THE CURRICULUM AND EXAMINATIONS (1965) Mathematics in Primary Schools, Curriculum Bulletin 1, London, HMSO

SCRIVEN, M. (1967) The methodology of evaluation, in R. Stake (ed.) Perspectivies of curriculum evaluation, Chicago, Rand McNally

SEYMOUR, W.D. (1937) An experiment showing the superiority of a light coloured blackboard. British Journal of Educational Psychology, 7, 259-268

SMITH, G. and WYLLIE, J.H. (1965) Use of closed circuit television in teaching surgery to medical students. British Medical Journal, 1965 (2), 99-101

SMITH, G., WYLLIE, J.H., FOOTE, A.V. and CARDIS, D.T. (1966) Further studies on the use of closed circuit television in teaching surgery to undergraduate students. British Journal of Medical Education, 1, 40-42

SOCKET, H. (1971) Bloom's taxonomy : a philosophical critique. Cambridge Journal of Education, 1, 16-25

SPENCER, H. (1861) Education: intellectual, moral and physical, London, Williams and Norgate

STALNAKER, J. (1951) in Lindquist, E.F. (ed.) Educational measurement, Washington, American Council of Education

STAVERT, G.S. and WINGATE, T.H. (1966) Nelson's Navy needed none but....'. Tutor Age, 17, 2-7

STEINBERG, H. and LEWIS, H.E. (1951) An experiment on the teaching value of a scientific film. British Medical Journal, 1951 (2), 465-467

STEUBNER, E.A. and JOHNSON, R.P. (1969) A hospital clerkship programme for dental students : an exploratory study. Journal of Dental Education, 32 (2), 224-229

STONES, E. and ANDERSON, D. (1970) Objectives and the teaching of educational psychology, Birmingham University School of Education

TAYLOR, R.G. and HANSON, G.R. (1969) Pre-college mathematics - workshop and freshmen achievement. Journal of Educational Research, 64 (3), 157-160

TEATHER, D.C.B. (1968) Programmed learning in biology. Journal of Biology Education, 2, 119-135

TRENAMAN, J.M. (1967) Communication and comprehension, London, Longmans, Green

UNIVERSITIES QUARTERLY (1967) Examining in universities. Universities Quarterly, 21 (3)

VALVERDI, H.H. and MORGAN, R.L. (1970) Influence on student achievement of redundancy in self-instructional materials. Programmed Learning and Educational Technology, 7 (3), 194-199

VERNON, P.E. (1946) An experiment on the value of the film and film-strip in the instruction of adults. British Journal of Educational Psychology, 16, 149-162

VERNON, P.E. (1961) The structure of human abilities 2nd edition, London, Methuen

WALL, G.I. (1967) The concept of vocational education, in Proceedings of the Annual Conference of the Philosophy of Education Society of Great Britain, 1967, 51-65

WALLIS, D. et al. (1966) Programmed instruction in the British armed forces, London, HMSO

WALLIS, D., DUNCAN, K.D. and KNIGHT, M.A.G. (1966) The Halton experiment and the Melksham experiment in programmed learning in the British armed forces, London, HMSO

WALTER, W.G. (1961) The living brain, Harmondsworth, Penguin

WALTON, H.J. and DREWERY, J. (1964) Teaching psychiatry to undergraduate medical students. Journal of Medical Education, 39 (6), 545-552

WALTON, H.J. and DREWERY, J. (1966) Psychiatrists as teachers in medical schools. British Journal of Psychiatry, 112, 489, 839-846

WEITZENHOFFER, A.M. (1953) Hypnotism : an objective study in suggestibility, New York, Wiley

WILLIAMS, E.R. and WOODING, E.R. (1968) The postgraduate education of physicists. Physics Education, 3 (3), 152-156

WILSON, G.M., LEVER, R., HARDEN, R.McG., ROBERTSON, J.I.S. and MacRITCHIE, J. (1969) Examination of clinical examinations. Lancet, 1969 (1), 37-40

WOODWORTH, R.S. (1922) Psychology (1st edition), London, Methuen

WRIGHT, E. (1968) A research project for clinical medical students, in Innovations and experiments in university teaching methods, report of the third conference organized by the University Teaching Methods Research Unit, Department of Higher Education, University of London Institute of Education, April 1968

ZORAB, J.S.M. and the DEPARTMENT OF AUDIO-VISUAL COMMUNICATION (1972) The management of cardiac arrest: Examination of the heart – an aspect of auscultation; Quantitative aspect of renal function, BMA with the British Life Assurance Trust for Health Education, Edinburgh, Churchill Livingstone